A STANDARD OF EXCELLENCE

ANDREW W. MELLON FOUNDS THE

NATIONAL GALLERY OF ART

AT WASHINGTON

Andrew W. Mellon

A Standard of Excellence

ANDREW W. MELLON FOUNDS THE

NATIONAL GALLERY OF ART AT WASHINGTON

BY DAVID EDWARD FINLEY

David Edward Finley

Smithsonian Institution Press   City of Washington   1973

Smithsonian Publication Number 4825
Copyright © 1973 by the Smithsonian Institution
All rights rerserved

Published in the United States by the Smithsonian Institution Press.
Distributed in the United States and Canada by George Braziller, Inc.,
and in all other countries by Feffer and Simons, Inc.

Designed by Elizabeth Sur
Printed in the United States by A. Colish, Inc.

Frontispiece photograph
by Bachrach; all other
illustrations by courtesy of
the National Gallery
of Art, Washington, D. C.

Library of Congress Cataloging in Publication Data
Finley, David E.
A standard of excellence.
(Smithsonian publication, no. 4825)
1. United States. National Gallery of Art.
2. Mellon, Andrew William, 1855-1937. I. Title.
N856.F56   708'.153   73-5676
ISBN O-87474-132-7

TO MY WIFE

MARGARET EUSTIS FINLEY

Contents

List of Illustrations

Foreword

Many people, particularly those of later generations, are apt to take their blessings, such as an art museum, for granted. They do not know, and cannot be expected to know, how such institutions were created and by whom and the difficulties which were encountered. For this reason it has seemed to me worthwhile to record my personal recollections of Andrew W. Mellon's successful efforts to establish a National Gallery to which others could contribute, and of its devlopment as a living, growing organism of the arts.

To do this I have written an account of some of Mr. Mellon's activities in his Washington years when he came to his decision to build a National Gallery of Art. In order to understand how this Gallery came into existence, it is necessary to know something of Mr. Mellon himself, his love of beauty, and his practical abilities in evolving a plan of this magnitude. Also I would like the public to know something of Mr. Mellon's personality, as I knew it and as his family and friends knew it. It is for this reason that I have mentioned several incidents, such as Mr. Mellon's speech to the Mayor of Southampton, his visit to the wine merchant in Bordeaux, and his meeting with Mr. Edison.

It was my good fortune to help in carrying out Mr. Mellon's ideas for the National Gallery, both during his lifetime and afterwards. I have told how I became involved in Mr. Mellon's undertaking and have tried to give some idea of the development of the National Gallery during the time I was Director (1938–1956).

I have confined this book to the subjects mentioned above. It is not an account of Mr. Mellon's activities or of mine, except as they relate to the founding of the National Gallery and its development in its

Mall entrance to the National Gallery of Art

early years, including its influence on the establishment of institutions, such as the National Portrait Gallery and others.

It should never be forgotten that it was Mr. Mellon's patriotism, his intelligence, and his generosity that brought the National Gallery of Art into being, and that his gifts of works of art, together with those of other donors, have made the National Gallery one of the great art museums of the world.

D. E. F.

Washington, October 1971

Author's note: Many of the conversations recorded in this book are not verbatim accounts but are reconstructed by me from notes made at the time, or while the conversations were still fresh in my memory.

Part 1

Miracle on the Mall

March 17, 1941, was a cold, blustery day in Washington. In the evening a high wind added to everyone's discomfort. But it did not deter over nine thousand persons from going to the opening of the National Gallery of Art on the Mall at Sixth Street. The audience, one of the most distinguished ever brought together in Washington, included The President and Mrs. Franklin Roosevelt and his Cabinet, the Supreme Court, the Congress, the Diplomatic Corps, and art collectors and trustees and directors of art museums from all parts of the country.

The beautiful marble building had been provided by Andrew W. Mellon, who gave his collection of paintings and sculpture as the nucleus of what he hoped would become a great national collection. There was also a large and important collection of paintings and sculpture given by Samuel H. Kress and the Samuel H. Kress Foundation, thus proving, at the very beginning, Mr. Mellon's belief that a beautiful building with works of art of the highest quality would attract similar gifts from other patriotic Americans.

Mr. Mellon was not there to see the miracle which he had created on the Mall. He had died in 1937. But his ideas had been carried out exactly as he wished. For over fifty years he had collected works of art, first for his own enjoyment in his home in Pittsburgh, and, after he had become Secretary of the Treasury, for a National Gallery of Art, which he considered to be a necessity in the capital of a country such as the United States of America. Nothing like this had ever happened before; and it happened then only because there sat in the Cabinet of a President of the United States a man with an extraordinary knowledge of practical matters, with a great love of beauty, and a self-effacing personality. He also had the resources and the generosity to carry out his plans.

In founding the National Gallery of Art in Washington, Andrew W. Mellon succeeded not only in giving to his country a much-needed, government-owned museum with an important collection of paintings and sculpture, to which others could contribute, but he also succeeded in establishing a standard of excellence in art and in making adherence to that standard mandatory, by Act of Congress,* insofar as the National Gallery is concerned.

Mr. Mellon's intention was to establish a National Gallery in Washington, not just another museum. He had in mind the National Gallery in London, the Louvre in Paris, and other great national museums, with standards of quality in works of art and efficiency in operation which he hoped would be realized in Washington.

The National Gallery is fortunate not only in having a standard of quality but also as regards the timing and circumstances under which it came into existence. It was the last possible moment when such a thing could have happened. The Mellon, Kress, Widener, Dale, and Rosenwald Collections were, with a few exceptions, the only ones remaining in private ownership that could, by coming together, create at once a National Gallery worthy of this country. Even so, it did seem miraculous that, in less than three years after the National Gallery was opened, it had become one of the great art museums of the world.

In addition to timing and circumstances, it was necessary also that Mr. Mellon, or someone as farseeing and self-effacing as he was, should erect a building and give a collection important enough to attract to Washington other donations of works of art of similar

---

* House Joint Resolution 217, section 5 (b), 75th Congress, specifies that "In order that the Collection of the National Gallery of Art shall always be maintained at a high standard and in order to prevent the introduction therein of inferior works of art, no work of art shall be included in the permanent collection of the National Gallery of Art unless it be of similar high standard of quality to those in the collection acquired from the donor [Mr. Mellon]."

quality. It was a rare combination of circumstances and it was owing to Mr. Mellon that advantage was taken of this opportunity.

There were many great art collections in this country to be seen in museums in New York, Boston, Philadelphia, Chicago, and other cities. But, with the exception of William Wilson Corcoran and Duncan Phillips, both of Washington, and Charles Lang Freer, of Detroit, no one had been interested in providing for the capital of this country an art gallery, containing the works of the greatest masters adequately housed in its own building.

When Mr. Mellon came to Washington in 1921 as Secretary of the Treasury, there was still no important collection of paintings and sculpture by the greatest masters of Western art owned by the federal government. The Corcoran Gallery of Art was founded by Mr. Corcoran in 1859 and a building was erected at Seventeenth Street and Pennsylvania Avenue, which was used by the United States Army from 1861 to 1869. It was then returned to the Corcoran Gallery trustees and the building and its collection, with an endowment from Mr. Corcoran, was opened to the public. Mr. Corcoran's object was to provide a center of American art in Washington and to encourage American artists. He was particularly interested in American art. This policy has been continued with the result that the gallery contains one of the most distinguished and comprehensive collections of American paintings, sculpture, and drawings to be found anywhere in the country. It also contains the Clark Collection of European paintings and fine examples of the decorative arts. The Corcoran Gallery holds frequent loan exhibitions of contemporary and earlier paintings, and maintains a well-attended art school.

The Phillips Collection, established by Duncan Phillips in his home in 1920, is also a private endowment. It contains a famous collection of modern art and its sources, chosen with great discrimination by Duncan and Marjorie Phillips. It includes many masterpieces, such as Renoir's *Le Déjeuner des Canotiers,* considered by many to be Renoir's greatest painting.

The Freer Gallery, which is an organization in the Smithsonian Institution, contains a superb collection of Oriental and Near-Eastern art, together with works by Whistler and a few other American artists. The works of art and the beautiful building that houses them were given by Mr. Freer; and he also provided an endowment for the purchase of additions to the Collection.

There was also an organization in the Smithsonian Institution, then known as the "National Gallery of Art," which is now known as "The National Collection of Fine Arts." It contained three collections, then shown as units, which included works by European and American artists and many objects of the decorative arts. There was also a fine group of paintings by the well-known American artist, Albert Pinkham Ryder, as well as paintings by nineteenth and early twentieth century artists which could serve as the basis for a museum of American contemporary art and its sources, under government auspices, as it is doing now in the beautiful old Patent Office Building which it shares with the newly established National Portrait Gallery. But it could not, by reason of the variety of its works of art, have served, in Mr. Mellon's opinion, as a foundation for a National Gallery containing paintings and sculpture by the greatest masters of Western art, such as he had in mind.

Mr. Mellon determined, therefore, to give his collection to the federal government and to offer to erect a building to house it and other works of similar quality, which might be given to the people of the United States. It was a wise decision. The building without his collection, or the collection without the building, would not have produced a National Gallery such as Mr. Mellon wished to establish.

II

Treasury Years

I had the good fortune to be in the Treasury Department when Mr. Mellon came to his great decision. I had gone there in 1922 as a member of the War Loan Staff, which consisted of five lawyers to whom a variety of duties was assigned. I had not met Mr. Mellon when I joined the War Loan Staff, and it was at the invitation of Parker Gilbert, the Under Secretary, that I came to the Treasury. He, himself, had come during the First World War as an assistant to Russell Leffingwell, Assistant Secretary of the Treasury. When the Wilson Administration ended, Mr. Leffingwell went back to New York. Parker Gilbert remained at the Treasury and was there when the new Secretary, Andrew W. Mellon, arrived on the scene in 1921.

Mr. Mellon recognized that, in Parker Gilbert and the others on the permanent staff, the Treasury had the best and most efficient organization to be found in any part of the government. They were completely loyal, first of all, to the Treasury and its integrity and then to its head, whether he be McAdoo or Glass or Mellon, as the new Secretary was to find later, to his own comfort and to the country's best interest. He determined at all costs to maintain the Treasury organization intact. He retained and made his Under Secretary that remarkable young man, Parker Gilbert, who later became Agent-General for Reparations in Berlin and subsequently a partner in J. P. Morgan and Company in New York. Parker Gilbert's invitation to me to join the War Loan Staff marked a turning point in my life.

I was to stay at the Treasury for ten years and I could not have found more interesting work or more satisfactory people with whom to work. When Parker Gilbert left for Berlin, Garrard Winston became Under Secretary and was succeeded by Ogden Mills, both men of great ability and devoted to the Treasury and to the public interest.

The wartime tax structure was badly in need of reform and Mr. Mellon had proposed certain ideas known as the "Mellon Tax Plan," which the Treasury was advocating. These ideas were incorporated in a book, *Taxation: The People's Business,* by Andrew W. Mellon, which he published in 1924 in order to bring about a better understanding of Treasury policy on taxation.

The five lawyers on the War Loan Staff prepared letters, speeches, and public statements about taxation, foreign loans, and other matters. The man who handled statements and correspondence about taxation decided that he did not agree with Treasury policy. He resigned, and his work was handed to me.

The work brought me in contact with Mr. Mellon, who eventually created a new job in the Treasury with the title "Special Assistant to the Secretary," to which he appointed me. And so began a long and happy association for me with one of the most remarkable men of his time.

Mr. Mellon has been described by people who did not know him as a shy, silent man, not given to speech if he could avoid it. He was a reticent man but not shy, and he was a very forceful character. If he had nothing he wanted to say, he kept silent; and while he did not suffer fools gladly, he gave his full attention to anyone with whom he happened to be talking.

Actually he liked talking with anyone whom he knew well and trusted. Once he and I were going to Pittsburgh for a meeting. I asked some questions about the beginning of the Aluminum Company. He told me with great detail and went on to talk about other companies in which he was interested or had founded and from which he had resigned as chairman or director when he became Secretary of the Treasury. Suddenly, after several hours of conversation, largely by Mr. Mellon, I saw that we were coming into the Pittsburgh station and we hastily decamped.

Mr. Mellon had a dry but delightful sense of humor and a very infectious laugh. He disliked garrulity or serious talk that made no sense. He had a disconcerting way of saying "Why?" when someone had been making statements or proposing something to which not too much thought had been given. "It sounds well," he would say, "but it won't work." And he had long years of experience to back his judgment.

Aside from his work in the Treasury and occasional visits to Pittsburgh and Europe and the companionship of his son and daughter, Mr. Mellon chiefly enjoyed buying paintings for his apartment in Washington. He had brought to Washington from Pittsburgh in 1921, when he became Secretary of the Treasury, a collection of paintings mostly of the English, American, and Dutch Schools and all of the highest quality. They had been bought for only one purpose: to give him pleasure in looking at them in his house on Woodland Road in Pittsburgh. They included paintings by Gainsborough, Romney, Raeburn, Rembrandt, Cuyp, Hobbema, Hals, and others. They had been acquired one at a time, mostly from M. Knoedler and Company in New York, with whom Mr. Mellon had dealt for years and in whom he had great confidence. In its later dealings with Mr. Mellon, the Knoedler firm was usually represented by Charles R. Henschel, Carman Messmore, and William F. Davidson.

Mr. Mellon's career as a collector had begun many years earlier. As a young man in his father's banking house, T. Mellon and Sons in Pittsburgh, Mr. Mellon had met a rising young industrialist, Henry Clay Frick, who had come there to discuss a business matter with Mr. Mellon's father. Mr. Frick became a friend of Andrew Mellon and interested him in paintings.

Later the two young men and a third friend were to make their first trip to Europe together. Either then, or on a later trip, Mr. Mellon brought home a painting for which he had paid a thousand dollars. He never identified the painting to me, but I understood that it had disappeared from the Mellon Collection long before its owner came to Washington. Mr. Mellon told me that his father's friends were rather horrified that he, Andrew Mellon, a young man of sense and judgment, should have paid so much money for a painting. But the younger Mellon persisted and, as his means permitted, he bought better paintings so that, when he came to Washington, his collection contained only fine examples of the work of great masters.

But there was no thought in the Pittsburgh years of a National Gallery. Mr. Mellon was happy in his work as president of banks and director of companies that were building up the industrial resources of the United States through development of oil, steel, abrasives, and aluminum.

It was with reluctance that Mr. Mellon gave up his lifework in Pittsburgh to come to Washington in 1921 as Secretary of the Treasury in President Harding's Cabinet. I always understood that he came at the urging of Senator Philander C. Knox of Pennsylvania and, so far as I know, Mr. Mellon never regretted it. He found himself in the Cabinet with some very distinguished associates, such as the Secretary of State, Charles Evans Hughes, and the Secretary of Commerce, Herbert Hoover. At the death of President Harding, Vice President Coolidge became head of the government and in him Mr. Mellon found a firm and understanding friend.

When Mr. Mellon became Secretary of the Treasury in 1921, the country was struggling under an intricate and burdensome tax structure inherited from World War I. Mr. Mellon insisted upon a reduction of expenditures and also a reduction of the public debt, which then amounted to twenty-four billion dollars and was, in his judgment, excessive. So there was no time to think of a National Gallery. Mr. Mellon was kept sufficiently busy trying to balance debt reductions with tax reductions and to evolve a system of taxation more suited to existing conditions.

Another absorbing interest arose. The government had outgrown existing buildings and badly needed new housing in Washington, such as can be found today in the Triangle group of buildings on the north side of Constitution Avenue from Fifteenth to Sixth Street. Congress realized that something must be done and in 1926 appropriated funds to initiate a plan for erecting the buildings needed. The Office of the Supervising Architect was then a bureau of the Treasury, so the responsibility for carrying out the plan for public buildings was placed on the Secretary of the Treasury.

Mr. Mellon enlisted the services of Charles S. Dewey, Acting Under Secretary of the Treasury, in organizing this work. Mr. Dewey secured the assistance of Edward H. Bennett of Chicago, a well-known architect, who became Consulting Architect of the Treasury and Chairman of the group of distinguished architects who designed the buildings in the Triangle area. Each architect was assigned one building and at frequent intervals they met together with Mr. Mellon, Mr. Dewey, and Mr. Bennett, so that the architects' designs, while having an individual character, were in harmony with each other. The rather shabby street bordering the Triangle on the south became Constitution Avenue connecting the Capitol with the Potomac River.

In order to place these plans before Congress, Mr. Mellon arranged a meeting to which he invited the Senators and Congressmen and the members of the American Institute of Architects, then assembled in Washington for their annual convention. The meeting was held in the evening of April 25, 1929, in the United States Chamber of Commerce building in Washington, when a model of the proposed buildings was placed on view. Also there was a motion picture, which Mr. Mellon had authorized me to have made at his expense, showing the future site of the Triangle buildings in all its shabbiness and as it would appear when the plans under way were carried out. Mr. Mellon presided at the meeting; President Hoover spoke, as did Senator Reed Smoot, Chairman, Public Buildings Commission; Congressman Richard N. Elliott, Chairman, House Committee on Public Buildings and Grounds; and Milton B. Medary, member of the National Capital Park and Planning Commission. So much interest was aroused that a similar meeting, with different speakers, was held on the following evening. Congress later gave its approval to these plans and appropriated the funds for carrying them out. The buildings were erected, composing one of the largest groups of public buildings ever constructed at one time in the history of the country.

While all this was going on, Mr. Mellon was revolving in his mind plans for a National Gallery of Art, which he felt to be a necessity in the capital of a great country such as the United States of America.

He had been embarrassed when representatives of foreign countries had come to the Treasury in Washington for debt settlements and other matters and had asked to be taken to "the National Gallery" where they could see some of the great paintings they knew were in this country. Mr. Mellon would reply that there was no such National Gallery of old masters, but that he had a few paintings in his apartment which he would be glad to show his visitors.

This situation gave rise, during the twenties and early thirties, to discussions about providing a building and improving the collection of the then National Gallery of Art which was housed in a few rooms in the Natural History Building, and is now known as the National Collection of Fine Arts. Dr. Charles Walcott and Dr. Charles G. Abbot of the Smithsonian Institution were greatly interested in the possibility of such a building, as were Senator Reed Smoot, Frederick A. Delano, Charles Moore, and various architects, who proposed sites on the Mall and elsewhere for the building to be erected, it was hoped, with funds provided by Mr. Mellon.

Meanwhile Mr. Mellon was making his own plans to erect a handsome building and to give his collection of works of art for a National Gallery of Art which he hoped to establish. He was encouraged to do this by those mentioned above and many others. I do not know how early he came to a definite decision, but he told me about his plans in 1927, and said that he hoped that I would stay on at the Treasury and help him to organize the new gallery which he expected to establish.

III

Life at the Treasury Was Never Dull

The realization of these plans was delayed by other matters that were demanding attention. President Coolidge had announced that he "did not choose to run" for re-election as President, and Mr. Mellon, who had been elected in May 1928 as Chairman of the Pennsylvania Republican Delegation to the Republican Convention to be held in Kansas City, would have great influence in the nomination of the candidate. The Secretary of Commerce, Herbert Hoover, was the leading contender, and Mr. Mellon expected to vote for him if President Coolidge or Charles Evans Hughes could not be induced to make the race. Under the circumstances, Mr. Mellon could not take a public position until the Pennsylvania delegation held a caucus in Kansas City and came to a decision.

Mr. Mellon asked me if I would like to go to Kansas City with him, which I was delighted to do. We travelled in a private Pullman car to Pittsburgh, where his brother, Richard B. Mellon, and his nephew, W. L. Mellon, came on board, and finally we all settled down in the Muehlebach Hotel in Kansas City. A stream of people came to Mr. Mellon's rooms, asking for his support for themselves or their candidates. Senator Charles Curtis of Kansas came and asked Mr. Mellon to support him for President. Mr. Mellon said no, he would be glad to support him for Vice President. Senator Curtis walked out, saying he did not want to be Vice President. Mr. Mellon, who was an excellent poker player, said to me with a smile, "He will take it just the same." Next day Mr. Mellon announced that the Pennsylvania delegation would vote for Hoover and Curtis, who were duly nominated and elected.

Mr. Mellon, his brother, nephew, and I came back to Pittsburgh in the private car. Mr. Mellon and I went on to Washington. Mr. Mellon was tired and decided to go to Europe for a short rest. His daughter, Mrs. Ailsa Mellon Bruce, and her husband, David Bruce, were going to a ranch in one of our Western states, and Paul Mellon was travelling in Europe with two of his Yale friends, so Mr. Mellon said to me: "I am going to Dinard and you are going to Europe for your holiday. Why don't you go to Dinard with me and then go on to Italy and the other places you like?" I was delighted with the idea, for I enjoyed Mr. Mellon's company and he treated me and his other younger friends as though we were all the same age.

Mr. Mellon's nephew, William Larimer Mellon, and his wife, and their son and daughter were to be on board the ship for a stay on the Brittany Coast. At Cherbourg, Mr. Mellon and I left the ship, going to Dinard where we remained for three weeks. We motored to Mont Saint-Michel and other places in the neighborhood; and finally Mr. Mellon realized a long-cherished desire to visit La Rochelle and see the subsidiary of the Standard Steel Car Company (which was a Mellon enterprise) making steel sleeping cars for the Wagon-Lits Company. William Larimer Mellon and his son Larimer, Paul Mellon and his friends, also Theodore Rousseau of the Guaranty Trust Company in Paris joined us at Dinard, and in three big motor cars we all went to La Rochelle and thoroughly inspected the steel sleeping cars that were being made there.

Then we motored to Lormont, near Bordeaux, where Mr. Mellon realized another ambition—to meet a Frenchman, Paul Mellon, son of André Mellon, a famous wine merchant, who had written to Mr. Mellon at Washington, telling of the strange coincidence of their names. Finally we reached the Rue André Mellon in Lormont and found the house of the French Paul Mellon, who, with his wife, received us most hospitably and, after seating us in a circle in the living room, offered us warm lemonade. The day was hot; there was apparently no ice in Lormont; and we had expected at least a taste of some of our host's fine vintage wines. In the end, the French Mr. Mellon offered us some brandy, which was part of his wife's dowry and very potent, so the day ended in a glow of satisfaction for all of us.

Mr. Mellon and I went back to Dinard and he decided to go to London with me for a few days. Then we went to Washington, having had, from my point of view, a very restful summer and, from Mr. Mellon's, a very exciting one, having seen not only the French Paul Mellon but all those Mellon-made steel sleeping cars at La Rochelle.

Life at the Treasury was never dull. In the summer of 1928 Congress had authorized the striking of a medal "commemorative of the achievements of Thomas A. Edison in illumining the path of progress through the development and application of inventions that have revolutionized civilization in the last century." Mr. Mellon, as Secretary of the Treasury, was directed to cause the medal to be made and to present it to Mr. Edison, which Mr. Mellon was delighted to do.

I got together some data about Mr. Edison and his achievements for Mr. Mellon to include in the speech he was to make over the radio in delivering the medal to Mr. Edison. All this involved long-distance telephone conversations with Charles Edison, Mr. Edison's son, who invited Mr. Mellon to dine with his parents before the ceremony and asked me to come, too.

On October 20, 1928, Mr. Mellon and I arrived at the Edison house, at Llewellyn Park near West Orange, New Jersey. Owing to a motorcycle escort from New York, we arrived early, so we had an opportunity to talk with Mr. Edison before the other guests came. Mrs. Edison gave me a pad and told Mr. Mellon and me to sit down beside her husband and write anything we wanted to ask him, as he was quite deaf.

After dinner we went to the famous Edison laboratory, where a large and distinguished group had gathered to hear President Coolidge speak to Mr. Edison over the radio and then to hear Mr. Mellon's speech in presenting the medal. "Few men," Mr. Mellon said, "in the history of the world have effected profound changes not only in the lives of their contemporaries but of all succeeding generations.

Thomas A. Edison is one of this small and illustrious company. In the space of a single lifetime, he has changed the conditions under which men live; and, more than anyone else now living, has helped to bring about a new social order, based on the achievements of modern science."

Ronald Campbell, Counselor of the British embassy at Washington, followed with a short speech, returning to Mr. Edison the original phonograph which had been on loan for years to the South Kensington Museum in London.

Dr. John Grier Hibben, President of Princeton University, made an eloquent speech in behalf of science and industry and all that Mr. Edison's achievements had meant to the world.

Copies of these speeches had been given to Mr. Edison, so that he could read them as they were being delivered. Mr. Edison was obviously pleased with all that had been said about him, and replied in the fewest possible words, for he made no speeches. When he had finished, he turned around and with a very delightful boyish gesture, threw out his hands and said, "That's all." Mr. Mellon and I agreed that we had never met a man to whom we had taken such a liking at first sight as we had to Mr. Edison.

The summer of 1931 was a very eventful one for me. I married Margaret Eustis on June 10th in the octagonal drawing room of Oatlands House in Loudoun County, Virginia, where her mother, Mrs. William Corcoran Eustis, went from Washington to spend the spring and autumn months. We went to England and before coming home went to Greece. Mr. Mellon was expecting us to stay a few days with him on the French Riviera, but in Brussels a telegram came from him asking us to join him in Paris and go to London to consult with the British Government and others as to what could be done about the financial situation.

The Credit-Anstalt Bank in Vienna had failed, precipitating serious results, as Mr. Mellon was well aware, in the international banking situation of our allies and their war-debt settlements with the United States. Mr. Mellon had received a telephone call from Ogden Mills, asking Mr. Mellon, at the request of President Hoover, to meet the Secretary of State, Henry Stimson, in Paris and go to London to confer with the British Government and others as to the best course to pursue.

We met Mr. Mellon in Paris and with Mr. and Mrs. Stimson and Theodore Marriner of our embassy in Paris, an old friend of ours, crossed to London and settled down in the Hyde Park Hotel.

I went every day for about a week with Mr. Stimson, Mr. Mellon, Theodore Marriner, Ray Atherton, and others in our London embassy to the British Foreign Office where the meetings were held. I remember one of the German delegates saying in an impassioned voice that if we didn't help Germany, the German people would turn to Hitler. To some of us it seemed incredible that anyone would precipitate a Second World War. A moratorium on reparations was approved and Germany was given time to set her finances in order, so that reparations and debt payments might be resumed. But it was all to no purpose, and we finally got Hitler and the chaos that followed World War II.

IV

Mr. Mellon Collects Paintings

During all these years Mr. Mellon continued to buy paintings, first for his apartment, and later for the National Gallery which he hoped to establish in Washington. Lord Duveen had met Mr. Mellon and achieved his ambition of selling him a few paintings. After that, it was a competition between Knoedler's and Duveen as to who could sell Mr. Mellon the best works of art.

Their method was to bring a painting to Washington, show it to Mr. Mellon, and then hang it on the walls of his apartment at 1785 Massachusetts Avenue, where it remained for two or three months in order that Mr. Mellon could make up his mind at leisure. Mr. Mellon had an unerring eye for quality in paintings and impeccable taste. He made his decisions after careful thought; but he liked to talk things over with someone whom he trusted and who could approach the matter with only Mr. Mellon's interest in mind. It was here that my usefulness to Mr. Mellon arose, insofar as art was concerned.

I usually went abroad every summer for my holiday and so became familiar with paintings in various museums and private collections in Europe as well as in this country. I had read art history and always preferred art to law, which I had studied at my father's suggestion, during the years we lived in Washington when he served as a Congressman from South Carolina. I shall only add that I never regretted my legal training, which was to prove of great value to me in later years, and was the bridge that led me to the Treasury.

Mr. Mellon often took me to lunch with him in his apartment on the top floor of 1785 Massachusetts Avenue when Charles Henschel or Carman Messmore of Knoedler's or Lord Duveen had brought a

Francisco de Goya, The Marquesa de Pontejos, *Andrew W. Mellon Collection*

painting in the hope that Mr. Mellon would become accustomed to it and buy it. When Mr. Mellon asked what I thought of the painting, I always gave him my honest opinion and my reasons for it, but I never urged him to buy anything he did not like, regardless of the importance of the painting, since he was buying for his own pleasure in the early years, at least, before he made plans for a National Gallery.

To many people the making of a great collection represents only a combination of money and luck. These elements are usually necessary, but there is far more to it than that. To make a really great collection, the collector must have taste, the ability to recognize quality, and perseverance in getting the best works of art obtainable in his field or period. All of these elements were present in the making of the Mellon Collection.

Mr. Mellon had some lucky breaks, but he also had the determination to take advantage of opportunities as they arose. A case in point was his acquisition of the full-length portrait of *The Marquesa de Pontejos* by Goya.

One day in February 1931, I had a telephone call from Miss Mary Patten, a friend of Mr. Mellon's, and also of mine, asking me to lunch next day. I had things to do at the Treasury and I said I couldn't leave. "You must," said Miss Patten. "It is about a famous Goya which Mr. Mellon can buy, and Mrs. Walter Schoellkopf, who is lunching here tomorrow, and whose husband is Counselor of the American embassy at Madrid, wants to tell you about it." So I dropped everything and at lunch next day Mrs. Schoellkopf said: "I was told that Mr. Mellon wanted an important painting by Goya and that he had asked particularly about one of a young man with yellow trousers. I know my friends in Spain are worried about the prospect of revolution. I am going back to Madrid now and if I find the painting can be bought, you must urge Mr. Mellon to act quickly."

Not long after that my telephone rang at the Treasury. It was Mrs. Schoellkopf calling from Madrid. "Mr. Mellon can have a far finer Goya than the one I spoke to you about. It is a full-length portrait of *The Marquesa de Pontejos y Miraflores*, and can be bought, I understand, for X number of dollars." I sent to the Library of Congress for an illustrated book of Goya's work and took it immediately to Mr. Mellon who was delighted with the Marquesa. He thought the matter over for a day or two. Another telephone call came from Mrs. Schoellkopf saying: "The family who own the portrait of *The Marquesa de Pontejos* are leaving Madrid tonight for Paris on the six o'clock train. Will you call me back at this number and tell me whether Mr. Mellon wants the painting and how high he will go?" I told Mr. Mellon about the call, and he said he would like to have the portrait if it could be managed in such a short time. I said that I had the telephone number in Madrid and we could call back. Mr. Mellon was greatly amused as I talked with Mrs. Schoellkopf and said that Mr. Mellon would like to buy the painting, giving a top limit. She cabled that the picture had been bought for slightly less than the limit and that Mr. Mellon would have to make his own arrangements about getting it out of Spain and that that would not be easy. Mr. Mellon telephoned Knoedler's in New York, asking that a man from their Paris office be sent to Madrid to arrange about payment and to apply for a permit for the export of the painting. The agent went there, the permit was given, and the painting duly arrived in Washington. Mr. Mellon was very happy about his purchase and always amused at having bought an important painting over the telephone. He was also very grateful to Mrs. Schoellkopf for her kindness in the matter.

Another case in which Mr. Mellon acted instantly and with determination was the acquisition of a fabulous group of paintings from the Hermitage Gallery in Leningrad. When the Bolshevik Government came to power in Russia, there were rumors that some of the works of art in the Hermitage might be sold. Finally, C. R. Henschel, of M. Knoedler and Company in New York, offered to go to Russia and buy for Mr. Mellon such paintings as might be offered for sale. Mr. Mellon authorized him to go and to submit such offers as he might receive. Mr. Henschel went to Russia and from time to time cables would arrive, saying that Botticelli's *Adoration of the Magi,* Jan van Eyck's *Annunciation,* Perugino's *Crucifixion,* Raphael's *Alba Madonna* and his *St. George and the Dragon,* Titian's *Venus with a Mirror,*

Botticelli, The Adoration of the Magi, *Andrew W. Mellon Collection*

Velázquez' study for his portrait of *Innocent X*, and several paintings by Rembrandt, van Dyck, and Frans Hals could be bought if Mr. Mellon approved. He gave his approval and Knoedler's secured twenty-one paintings which Mr. Mellon eventually agreed to buy. He did not announce these purchases because he wanted them to be seen first by the public in the National Gallery he expected to build.

The paintings from the Hermitage were stored in a large, unused room in the Corcoran Art Gallery, owing to the kindness of the trustees of that institution. The walls of the room were literally covered with masterpieces. Once a month Mr. Mellon and I would go to see them. The paintings were safe and there they remained until they were transferred to the National Gallery on the completion of the building, an event which Mr. Mellon was destined not to see.

Raphael, The Alba Madonna, *Andrew W. Mellon Collection*

Raphael, Saint George and the Dragon, *Andrew W. Mellon Collection*

25

Jan van Eyck, The
Annunciation,
Andrew W. Mellon Collection

Diego Velázquez, Pope Innocent X, *Andrew W. Mellon Collection*

Titian, Venus with a Mirror, *Andrew W. Mellon Collection*

V

London Interlude

In 1932 came a temporary halt to Mr. Mellon's collecting and to his plans for a National Gallery of Art. For more than a year he bought only one painting. The Depression had greatly increased Mr. Mellon's burdens as Secretary of the Treasury. President Hoover was aware of this and in the winter of 1932 asked Mr. Mellon whether he would like to go to England as the American ambassador. Mr. Mellon considered the matter carefully, taking into consideration the English climate, which did not agree with him. Finally he decided to accept, leaving the Treasury in the capable hands of his friend, Ogden Mills, the Under Secretary.

At the time Mr. Mellon came to his decision, my wife and I had gone to Boca Grande on the west coast of Florida for a winter holiday. We were at the moment gathering shells on the beach, when a telegram came from Mr. Mellon, saying that he had decided to accept the English mission; that he would like me to go with him; and asking us to return to Washington as soon as possible. We did so and the Department of State made me an attaché of embassy, with the honorary rank of Counselor.

We were sad to leave Washington, but were delighted to go to London and to live in a house, which we rented on Eaton Place, and to learn how the English coped with their problems, as one never learns in hotels.

Mr. Mellon, my wife, and I crossed in the *Majestic* in April 1932 arriving after dark on April 7 at Southampton. Ray Atherton, the able and distinguished Counselor of the embassy, came on board to meet Mr. Mellon. After talking for a few minutes, Ray pulled out of his pocket a short, typewritten speech. Handing it to Mr. Mellon, he said: "Tomorrow morning the Mayor of Southampton will come on board to greet you and I thought you might like to have this little speech to reply to him." Mr. Mellon read the speech, then looked at Ray: "It is very nice but it doesn't say anything new. Of course 'blood is thicker than water' and I am glad to be in England again but that has been said over and over. What is the point of my saying it again?" Ray looked rather puzzled: "Mr. Ambassador, is there anything you would particularly like to say to the Mayor of Southampton?" "Yes," said Mr. Mellon. "I would like to tell him about Mrs. Schenley who came from Pittsburgh and lived part of each year near Southampton." Ray looked more puzzled than ever, so I said, "Go to bed, Ray. Mr. Mellon and I know all about Mrs. Schenley and we will be ready for the Mayor of Southampton when he comes aboard tomorrow morning." So then Mr. Mellon composed a short speech about Mrs. Schenley, who was the grandmother of friends of mine and whom Mr. Mellon greatly admired because of her devotion to Pittsburgh.

Mrs. Schenley, as Mr. Mellon was to tell the Mayor of Southampton next morning, had lived in Pittsburgh, where she was said to be one of the greatest heiresses of her time. While she was a girl at boarding school, she met an Englishman, Captain Edward Schenley, who was, I understood, three times her age. In any event he fascinated her. She eloped with him, to her father's rage, and went to England, where she had a very happy life, dying, I was told, at the age of ninety, and leaving three children. One of the granddaughters, Mrs. Hemeleer-Schenley, had been a friend of mine for many years, so I knew all about the romantic story of her grandmother. Mrs. Schenley returned occasionally to Pittsburgh for visits and gave the land for Schenley Park which, as Mr. Mellon said in his remarks to the Mayor next morning, "is to Pittsburgh as Hyde Park is to London."

Mr. Mellon was delighted to be able to pay tribute to Mrs. Schenley and to say something "definite." Everyone was happy and when we got to London, Mrs. Hemeleer-Schenley telephond me that she could not have been more surprised "to find Grandmama on the pages of the *London Times* after all those many years."

This little incident was typical of Mr. Mellon and part of his charm. He was equally "definite" about all those speeches he made in London in the year following at the English-Speaking Union, The Pilgrims Society, the Mansion House, and many more. He was also courageous in standing up for America in a polite but firm manner. On one occasion, in speaking to the English-Speaking Union, he made the usual polite tribute to the dominant part which English civilization has had in the making of the United States of America. He then went on to praise the contribution made by those who have come from other countries and have merged their identity with our own. I was sitting next to an American-born Dowager Countess who listened with tears in her eyes. "I have lived here a long time," she said, "but I never expected to see an American ambassador with the courage to praise 'the foreign-born' in America, as they are called here."

Mr. Mellon was also quite definite on the subject of art. He took all his best paintings (the ones on canvas which would not be affected by removal to another climate) to decorate the walls of the embassy residence at Prince's Gate. And it is unnecessary to add that this house has never looked the same before or since.

Before Mr. Mellon left Washington, someone had said to him that the English might be embarrassed to find their ancestors on the walls of the American embassy, as painted by Gainsborough, Romney, Raeburn, and Lawrence. Mr. Mellon was not impressed, but he said to me, "You might inquire about it of your friends." So I went to Sir Ronald Lindsay, then British ambassador at Washington, who laughed heartily and said: "The only embarrassment Mr. Mellon will suffer will be in refusing to buy more paintings of British ancestors!"

Mr. Mellon determined for other reasons that he would buy no paintings while he was in London. "Buying a good painting takes time," he said, "and I shall have no time to give to such matters."

Then one day David Bruce made a suggestion which we all thought had great merit. He told Mr. Mellon of the portrait of

Pocahontas painted from life in 1616 when she and her English husband, John Rolfe, were visiting in London. The Indian Princess was dressed in the height of London fashion, and the painting is, of course, of great interest historically, especially to America. It was owned at the time by Francis Burton Harrison, former Congressman and Governor General of the Philippines, then living in Scotland, but at the moment in a nursing home in London. David Bruce had heard that Mr. Harrison might be willing to sell the portrait and Mr. Mellon agreed that he would like to buy it. "But there is my promise to myself, not to buy any paintings while I am Ambassador. If I make an exception now, there will be other cases that will arise to plague me."

At this point I spoke up. "I haven't made any promises of any kind. I know Mr. Harrison. If you will put enough money in the bank in my name to pay Mr. Harrison's price, I will go and talk with him." Mr. Mellon was amused and said to go ahead and talk with Mr. Harrison, which I did. Mr. Harrison said yes, he would sell the painting for X dollars. I said I would take it, secured Mr. Mellon's approval, and wrote out a check to Mr. Harrison for the amount agreed upon. My check was duly honored at the bank and *Pocahontas* came to the American embassy.

Mr. Mellon left the portrait, together with the Clarke Collection which he had acquired, containing about a hundred portraits by American artists, to the National Gallery, with the intention that some should become part of the Gallery's Collection, and others, mostly of historical interest, should go to a National Portrait Gallery if and when such a gallery should come into being. Now the National Portrait Gallery has been established by Congress. The portrait of *Pocahontas* is there to represent one of the earliest Americans who contributed to the history of this country. So are many other portraits, such as those in the Clarke Collection, which were provided by Mr. Mellon's foresight.

I serve now as a member of the National Portrait Gallery Commission, appointed by the Regents of the Smithsonian Institution;

and it gives me great satisfaction that this much needed history museum has at last come into existence.

The collection of portraits and archives are housed in the beautiful old Greek Revival building at Ninth and F Streets, formerly the Patent Office Building. The building was begun in 1837 and completed in 1867. It was the scene of many historical events, including the second Inaugural Ball of President Lincoln. The building was scheduled to be demolished to make way for a parking lot. The Commission of Fine Arts, of which I was chairman at the time, advised strongly that the building be preserved and used for a National Portrait Gallery. We met with some opposition in government offices. So I took the matter to The White House, and President Eisenhower ordered that the building be saved for a National Portrait Gallery. Senator Hubert H. Humphrey introduced a bill to preserve the building and a bipartisan committee of Senators and Representatives transferred the building to the Smithsonian Institution to house a National Portrait Gallery and the National Collection of Fine Arts, which have now been installed there.

V I

Collecting Continues

Mr. Mellon seemed to enjoy his year in London as Ambassador. He went frequently to the National Gallery, which he liked because of the high quality of its paintings and the way in which they were shown. He found many old friends in England and made many new ones. He also took great pride in the grace with which his daughter, Mrs. David Bruce, presided over the embassy residence.

In March 1933, at the end of the Hoover Administration, Mr. Mellon left London and returned to Washington and to his home in Pittsburgh. Donald Shepard and I formed a law firm in Washington. Don devoted himself, as before, to Mr. Mellon's legal interests in Washington, and I was concerned mostly with Mr. Mellon's plans for a National Gallery.

Mr. Mellon was obliged to devote much of his time during his remaining years to a tax case brought by the New Deal Administration for additional income taxes alleged to be due for the year 1931 as the result of a sale of stock. Without any demand by the Treasury for additional taxes and a hearing given, as provided by law, the Attorney General announced to the press that he was sending Mr. Mellon's case to the Grand Jury at Pittsburgh and asking for an indictment. The Grand Jury considered Mr. Mellon's case and refused to indict, returning the verdict "not a true bill," which ended the proceedings.

The Treasury renewed the charges and proposed to assess additional taxes. Mr. Mellon denied that any taxes were due; hearings, that lasted for months, were held at Pittsburgh before the Board of

Tax Appeals (now the United States Tax Court). The final argument
was made on June 11, 1936, but a decision was not announced until
after Mr. Mellon's death, when the Board, in a unanimous decision,
found the stock sale valid, but on other grounds of a technical nature
made an addition to Mr. Mellon's taxes for the year 1931, which was
paid by his estate. The result was considered a complete vindication
of Mr. Mellon.

Mr. Mellon did not allow this experience to embitter him. During
all this time he went ahead with his plans for a National Gallery; but
he waited until the tax hearings were concluded in June 1936 before
making public his offer of this great gift to the nation.

Some of his friends tried to deter him. "Why do you give your collection to Washington when you have been treated so badly by the
New Deal Administration?" Mr. Mellon replied firmly: "I am not
going to be deterred from building the National Gallery in Washington. Eventually the people now in power in Washington will be dead

and I will be dead, but the National Gallery, I hope, will be there and that is something the country needs."

New opportunities to acquire paintings came his way. The small but very important painting, *Nativity With the Prophets Isaiah and Ezekiel,* painted by Duccio di Buoninsegna between 1308 and 1311, for the predella at the front of the great altarpiece known as the *Maestá* for the Cathedral in Siena, had come into Duveen's hands. He had been taken sick while passing through Germany and had left the train. The next day he had called at the local museum to see the Director, who told him that he was going to Berlin as Director of the Kaiser Friedrich Museum. He said that Hitler had told him to get more paintings by German artists for that museum, and, if necessary, to exchange Italian works of art to that end. After Lord Duveen returned to New York, he wrote to the Director at Berlin, offering to exchange a German painting for the Duccio. The Director agreed; the Duccio arrived in New York; and in the spring of 1937 it became part of the Mellon Collection. Later, Samuel H. Kress was to add another Duccio from the same altarpiece, *The Calling of the Apostles Peter and Andrew,* now in the National Gallery.

Meanwhile some of my future colleagues had come to Washington for the meeting of the American Association of Art Museum Directors. They came to Mr. Mellon's apartment to see his paintings. I saw some of them looking at the Duccio and shaking their heads sadly over Mr. Mellon's having been taken in by a copy, until I assured them it was the original from the *Maestá* altarpiece and told how it came to Washington.

Another great piece of luck was Mr. Mellon's purchase in December 1936 of the Dreyfus Collection of Renaissance sculpture. It was a very famous collection and had been largely assembled by Charles Timbal who had sold the collection to Gustave Dreyfus. On the death of M. Dreyfus, the collection went to his daughters, who finally accepted Lord Duveen's offer of ten percent more than any other offer received. The collection came to New York, where Mr. Mellon and I saw it at the offices of Duveen Brothers, following Mr. Mellon's return from England in 1933.

Mr. Mellon had often talked with me about the Dreyfus Collection but he had never made up his mind to buy it. He had, however, acquired from Knoedler's the important marble bas-relief, *Madonna and Child* by Agostino di Duccio. Mr. Mellon had bought it in January 1935. This was the first piece of sculpture acquired by him for the collection destined for the National Gallery and was a happy augury of more to follow.

Mr. Mellon had gone to England in the summer of 1936 with his daughter, Mrs. David Bruce. My wife and I were in London when they arrived, and Mr. Mellon and I went to museums, and finally we went to Duveen Brothers to see what Lord Duveen had to offer. Lord Duveen was overjoyed to hear that Mr. Mellon felt that he was at last in a position to make his great gift of a National Gallery to the nation. "I have many masterpieces in New York which have been hidden in storage during the Depression," Duveen told Mr. Mellon. "You must come to see them when you get back to America. They will help to round out your collection before you give it to the country." Mr. Mellon said, yes, he would come, and eventually we all went back to America.

Mr. Mellon went to his house in Pittsburgh, expecting to come to Washington in October and to take me to New York with him to see Duveen's treasures. But Mr. Mellon was not well, so I went to Pittsburgh and spent some time with him in the Woodland Road house, going over the plans for the National Gallery. We would walk around the garden and his eyes would brighten as he talked about his last great project, which he was determined to put through as soon as possible.

I went back to Washington, and one night, after I had gone to bed with a heavy cold, the telephone rang. Mr. Mellon was on the line and said, "I don't feel well enough to go to New York and see Duveen and all those paintings. Will you go and bring back everything you think is good enough for the National Gallery. Then I will come to Washington and decide what I want to buy. I have telephoned Duveen and he will have everything in readiness for you to see." I said, "Certainly, I will go at once, but may I bring back the sculpture

Agostino di Duccio, Madonna and Child, *Andrew W. Mellon Collection*

in the Dreyfus Collection?" Mr. Mellon said, "Yes, bring back the sculpture, too." I took the midnight train and next morning was with Lord Duveen at 720 Fifth Avenue. We were there for the greater part of three days. Lord Duveen had his people bring into the velvet-hung room one painting and sculpture after another.

I had been told to bring back "everything I thought good enough for the National Gallery." So after much agonizing on my part, I settled on thirty paintings and twenty-one pieces of sculpture. The paintings were not only fine examples of the work of great artists, but were needed to fill the gaps in the Mellon Collection, so that it would give some idea of the achievements of Western painting from the thirteenth to the nineteenth century.

The earliest of the paintings was that of the *Enthroned Madonna and Child,* painted, according to Bernard Berenson, in Constantinople around the year 1200; there was a fine painting attributed to Cimabue, and still another was the large figure painting of *St. Paul,* which hangs in the National Gallery and is attributed to a follower of Giotto. Lord Duveen showed me the painting with a flourish, announcing it as by Giotto. I said: "I know the painting. Mr. Berenson says it is by 'A Follower of Giotto.'" Lord Duveen insisted, "I say it is by Giotto and it will be by Giotto." I said, "It is a fine painting and I think you might send it to Washington for Mr. Mellon to see. But, if he buys it, it will be as 'A Follower of Giotto.'" When I went back to Washington, I told Mr. Mellon the story. He smiled and said, "I will remember." And later when Mr. Mellon and Lord Duveen met in Washington to settle about the pictures, Mr. Mellon said firmly: "I will buy the *St. Paul* painting as 'A Follower of Giotto' and at a suitable price, not the price of a Giotto, and it will so hang in the National Gallery," as it does today, with an attribution to Giotto's follower, Bernardo Daddi. Other paintings which were brought to Washington at this time and were purchased by Mr. Mellon included works by Masaccio, Antonello da Messina, Neroccio de' Landi, Agnolo Gaddi, Lippo Memmi, Pisanello, Allegretto Nuzi, and others.

Twenty-one pieces of sculpture from the Dreyfus and other collections were also sent to Washington. They included Donatello's

Byzantine School, XIII Century, Enthroned Madonna and Child, *Andrew W. Mellon Collection*

Bust of St. John the Baptist; Desiderio da Settignano's marble *Bust of a Little Boy;* Verrocchio's bust of *Giuliano de'Medici,* and his *Putto Poised on a Globe;* Mino da Fiesole's bas-reliefs representing *Faith* and *Charity;* and Andrea della Robbia's *The Virgin Adoring the Child.* Other works which were sent to Washington at that time and bought by Mr. Mellon are the marble bust of *A Princess of the House of Aragon* by Laurana; the full-length bronze statues representing *Bacchus* and *Venus* by Sansovino, now in the West Sculpture Hall at the National Gallery, and the bronze statue of *Mercury* attributed to Adriaen de Vries, now at the top of the fountain in the rotunda of the National Gallery.

Lord Duveen rented an apartment, beneath Mr. Mellon's at 1785 Massachusetts Avenue, where he installed these treasures, with guards, so that Mr. Mellon could consider the works of art at his leisure. Every day Mr. Mellon would spend an hour or two looking at them. A few friends whose views Mr. Mellon valued, such as Duncan Phillips, were invited to see them; and, of course, his son Paul, his son-in-law David Bruce, and Donald Shepard, on all of whom Mr. Mellon relied to carry out his wishes about the National Gallery. Finally Mr. Mellon made up his mind. Of the thirty paintings he decided to buy twenty-four; of the twenty-one sculptures, eighteen. He asked me to telephone Lord Duveen and invite him to lunch. I was the only other person present, to watch these two keen minds at work and both enjoying the contest immensely. Lord Duveen asked astronomical prices. Mr. Mellon countered with lower ones. At one point Mr. Mellon said: "Well, Lord Duveen, I think you will have to take all these things back to New York," and Lord Duveen replied: "Mr. Mellon, I would give you these things for the National Gallery rather than take them away." Finally it was all settled; Mr. Mellon had everything he wanted, and both he and Lord Duveen were very happy at the outcome of the great transaction. By December 15, 1936, Mr. Mellon had largely concluded his purchases. His collection was by this time a very important one and quite adequate to become the nucleus of a great National Gallery, as Mr. Mellon hoped would be the case.

Desiderio da Settignano, Bust of a Little Boy, *Andrew W. Mellon Collection*

VII

The National Gallery Comes into Existence

Mr. Mellon selected a site on Constitution Avenue between Fourth and Seventh Streets for the museum building, which he expected to erect. But this site, unfortunately, had been allocated to the George Washington Memorial Association, of which Mrs. Henry Dimock was the president and principal benefactor. The Association had planned to erect a building on this site as a memorial to George Washington.

Excavations had been started, but sufficient funds were not forthcoming and the undertaking seemed to be at a standstill. One of the trustees was Mrs. Charles Hamlin, who was a friend of Mr. Mellon's and also of mine. I proposed to Mr. Mellon that I ask Mrs. Hamlin to talk with Mrs. Dimock and urge that she make the site available for the new art museum. Mrs. Hamlin was agreeable but rather reluctant to approach Mrs. Dimock with this suggestion. However, encouraged by Mr. Hamlin, she did so, and next morning telephoned me that Mrs. Dimock had been most understanding and had said, rather sadly, that she saw no prospects of completing their memorial and that she was quite willing to evacuate the site. Later the remaining funds of the Association were given to the George Washington University, and Mrs. Dimock and the Association, in a letter to the Committees of Congress, supported the plan to make the site available for the new art museum. In testifying before the House of Representatives Committee on the Library on February 17, 1937, A. K. Shipe introduced the letter in the record and the hurdle of locating a site was overcome.

But there were other hurdles. The Southwest Citizens Association of Washington passed a resolution opposing the closing of Sixth

Street across the Mall. The closing of the street there was necessary in order to provide a site large enough for the art museum as designed by John Russell Pope, who had been selected by Mr. Mellon as the architect for the building. The Secretary of the Southwest Citizens Association was a young lawyer, Harry S. Wender. I proposed to Mr. Mellon that I go to Mr. Wender and explain the situtation. I did so and found Mr. Wender very sympathetic when he understood the requirements of the architectual design and that the museum, which was to be 785 feet in length, could not be built on the proposed site unless Sixth Street was closed as it crossed the Mall. I took Mr. Wender the next afternoon to Mr. Mellon's apartment at 1785 Massachusetts Avenue when Mr. Mellon showed him Mr. Pope's rendering of the proposed National Gallery building, and I showed him some of the paintings that were to be exhibited in the Gallery. Mr. Wender was very understanding and later secured the approval of the Southwest Citizens Association and the Federation of Citizens Association to the closing of Sixth Street on the Mall, and he so testified before the House Committee when it was considering the matter.

Meanwhile Frederick A. Delano, Chairman of the National Capital Park and Planning Commission, brought the matter of the closing of Sixth Street before the members of his Commission, who agreed that any future increase in traffic, owing to the closing of Sixth Street, could be accommodated by the widening of Seventh and Ninth Streets; and Mr. Delano so testified before the House Committee.

The last hurdle was the matter of the name of the proposed gallery. The Smithsonian Institution had long been the custodian of the government's collections of history and science. It also was the custodian of the government's art collections, such as the Freer Gallery and the collection of paintings and other works of art then known as the National Gallery of Art. Mr. Mellon felt that it would be impossible to bring into existence a gallery of the kind he had in mind, based on the existing "National Gallery of Art," as then constituted. It was agreed, therefore, by the Regents of the Smithsonian Institution that the existing museum should be known as "The National Collection of Fine Arts," and the proposed new museum should be called "The National Gallery of Art."

The situation was in order now for Mr. Mellon to make his offer to the President, which he did in the following letter:

730 Fifteenth Street
Washington, D.C.

December 22, 1936.

The President
The White House

My dear Mr. President:

Over a period of many years I have been acquiring important and rare paintings and sculpture with the idea that ultimately they would become the property of the people of the United States and be made available to them in a national art gallery to be maintained in the city of Washington for the purpose of encouraging and developing a study of the fine arts.

I have within the last few years transferred these paintings and sculpture to trustees with responsibility for carrying out this purpose and have given them full power and authority to deed these works of art to a national gallery if and when such an institution shall assume and be prepared to carry out the purposes intended. In addition, I have given to the trustees securities ample to erect a gallery building of sufficient size to house these works of art and to permit the indefinite growth of the collection under a conservative policy regulating acquisitions.

Such a gallery would be for the use and benefit of the general public; and it is my hope that it may attract gifts from other citizens who may in the future desire to contribute works of art of the highest quality to form a great national collection. In connection, therefore, with the intended gift, I shall stipulate that the proposed building shall not bear my name, but shall be known as The National Art Gallery or by such other name as may appropriately identify it as a gallery of art of the National Government.

In order to carry out this purpose, and with the approval of the other trustees, I wish to propose a plan to give the art collection which I have brought together to the Smithsonian Institution or to the United States Government for the benefit of the people of this country, and also to erect or cause to be erected on public land a suitable building for a national gallery of art, the design and materials of which shall be subject to the approval of the Fine Arts Commission. Mr. John Russell Pope, of New York, has been employed as architect to study this project and will furnish designs for such a building.

The location of such a gallery is a matter that must be given most careful consideration. It should not only be readily accessible to those wishing to visit the gallery, but should also be located at a point with sufficient surrounding property, under control of public authorities, to protect it from undesirable encroachments. In my own opinion and that of others who are familiar with the general plan of Washington, it would seem that a site on the Mall would most nearly meet these requirements; and the designation of a definite site, therefore, for the building on public land will be incorporated in the offer of the gift to the Government.

In addition to the gift of the art collection and a building in which it and similar collections may be housed and displayed, I plan also to establish an endowment fund for the proposed gallery, the income from which shall be used to pay the annual salaries of a director, assistant director, secretary, and curators of the gallery, and for possible future art acquisitions. The upkeep of the building and other administrative expenses and costs of operation would be provided in appropriations to be made by Congress, as for the other units of the Smithsonian Institution.

The orderly and efficient administration of the proposed gallery and its policy respecting acquisitions are both imperative considerations affecting the establishment of such a gallery. I would suggest that the affairs of the proposed gallery should be managed by a competent and separate board of trustees acting for it as a unit of the Smithsonian Institution and that they be empowered to make bylaws and regulations governing its operations.

It is of the greatest importance that future acquisitions of works of art whether by gift or purchase, shall be limited to objects of the highest standard of quality, so that the collections to be housed in the proposed building shall not be marred by the introduction of art that is not the best of its type. I have tried to adhere to this standard in the collection which I have made. That collection is representative of most of the great masters of western Europe and includes outstanding works of art which I acquired from the Hermitage Gallery in Russia. It also contains Renaissance sculptures, including most of those formerly in the Dreyfus collection in Paris; and there is in addition, a large assemblage of American protraits from the Clarke and other collections, which would be suitable for a national portrait gallery.

By reason of the rarity and importance of these works of art, the general character of the collection is such that it will furnish the nucleus of a great national collection and will give our country at once a national gallery that will rank with the other great galleries of the world. In making the collection, I have placed emphasis on quality rather than quantity; and the terms under which the gift would be made are intended solely for the purpose of safeguarding the collection and insuring efficient management, so that the highest standard of quality will always be maintained in the art to be displayed in the gallery.

If this plan meets with your approval, I will submit a formal offer of gift stating specifically the terms thereof, and the erection of the building may proceed immediately upon the acceptance of such offer and the passage of necessary legislation by Congress. Appropriate instruments of conveyance and gift will then be executed.

Sincerely yours,
/s/ A. W. Mellon

I took the letter to Frederick Delano, the President's uncle and an old friend of Mr. Mellon. Mr. Delano, who knew of Mr. Mellon's plans, was delighted to be of help and said he would give the letter to the President personally next day when he was dining at The White House.

Mr. Mellon received immediately a very cordial letter from the President:

The White House
Washington, D.C.

December 26, 1936.

Hon. A. W. Mellon
730 Fifteenth Street
Washington, D.C.

My dear Mr. Mellon:

When my uncle handed me your letter of December 22 I was not only completely taken by surprise but was delighted by your very wonderful offer to the people of the United States.

This was especially so because for many years I have felt the need for a national gallery of art in the Capital. Your proposed gift does more than furnish what you call a "nucleus," because I am confident that the collections you have been making are of the first importance and will place the Nation well up in the first rank.

Furthermore, your offer of an adequate building and endowment fund means permanence in this changing world.

Because the formal offer calls for specific statement of the terms and will have to be worked out before any request is made by me to the Congress for the necessary legislation, may I suggest that you, or whoever you may care to designate, should come to see me some after-noon this week.

Also, I think that we should discuss the formal announcement and the terms of it.

With renewed appreciation of your letter, believe me

Very sincerely yours,
/s/ Franklin D. Roosevelt

Mr. Mellon said: "I would like to talk with the President about it." Knowing the excitement Mr. Mellon's presence at The White House would cause, I said: "Let me arrange for you to talk with the President in the Mansion," which I did. The President was delighted and asked Mr. Mellon to come to tea that afternoon in his library on the second floor of The White House, and would I come too. The President said he would have Mr. Cummings, the Attorney General, there in case he might be helpful about any legal questions that might arise.

Mr. Mellon and I went to The White House at five o'clock. We found Mr. Roosevelt seated on a sofa in front of the fire. He motioned Mr. Mellon to sit beside him and I sat near Mr. Cummings. The President turned on his charm, and he and Mr. Mellon were deep in conversation for some time. At last Mr. Mellon pulled a letter out of his pocket; "Here, Mr. President, is my offer. I hope it can be carried out."

In the letter he offered to erect a building for the National Gallery and to give his collection as the nucleus of a National Collection. He stipulated that the Gallery was not to bear his name and that, in addition to his collection, the Gallery was to exhibit other works of art of like quality which other citizens might in the future contribute to the National Gallery. He offered to give an endowment (five million dollars, later increased to ten million), the income to be used for the salaries of the five top gallery officials and for the purchase of paintings, etc., but not for the upkeep of the building and its personnel. That, he stipulated, should be paid by the government, as in other public buildings. He requested also that a site be set aside on the Mall at Sixth Street and Constitution Avenue, and that Congress should charter the National Gallery of Art, with its own trustees but as a unit of the Smithsonian Institution.

The President read the letter, apparently with pleasure, then tossed it to the Attorney General, asking whether there was any reason why the government could not do what Mr. Mellon had outlined in his letter. The Attorney General read the letter and said that the government could do everything requested in the letter. Then put it through, said Mr. Roosevelt, as Mr. Mellon has outlined in his letter. He added that it was a most generous offer and a wonderful thing for this country.

At that point, Miss Le Hand came in to pour tea, with some of the Roosevelt grandchildren to look on. We had a very pleasant time and finally Mr. Mellon arose to go. He thanked President Roosevelt for his help and we returned to Massachusetts Avenue.

Next day Mr. Mellon's Washington attorney, Donald Shepard, who had such an important role in all these negotiations, made a draft of legislation embodying the essential points that had been agreed upon. In consultation with representatives of the Department of Justice and the Smithsonian Institution, a bill was prepared and introduced in the Congress as House Joint Resolution 217. It was referred to the Senate Committee on Public Buildings and Grounds, of which Senator Tom Connally was Chairman, and to the House Committee on the Library, of which Congressman Kent E. Keller was Chairman. The proposed legislation was approved by the Bureau of the Budget and by the Treasury, and also by the Smithsonian Institution.

The bill stated that "the area bounded by Seventh Street, Constitution Avenue, Fourth Street and North Mall Drive, Northwest, in the District of Columbia is hereby appropriated to the Smithsonian Institution as a site for a National Gallery of Art." It provided also that "the adjoining area bounded by Fourth Street, Pennsylvania Avenue, Third Street and North Mall Drive, Northwest, in the District of Columbia, is hereby reserved as a site for future additions to the National Gallery of Art." The bill established the National Gallery of Art as a unit of the Smithsonian Institution, with its own Board of Trustees to be composed of the Chief Justice of the United States, the Secretary of State, the Secretary of the Treasury, and the Secretary of the Smithsonain Institution as trustees ex officio, and five general trustees who shall be citizens of the United States and shall be chosen, on first taking office, by the Regents of the Smithsonian Institution, subject to the approval of the donor, Mr. Mellon. Successors to the five general trustees were to be chosen by a majority of the general trustees, and were to serve for a period of ten years each. The bill stated that "the faith of the United States is pledged that, on the completion of the National Gallery of Art by the donor in accordance with the terms of this Act and the acquisition from the donor of the Collection of works of art, the United States will provide such funds as may be necessary for the upkeep of the National Gallery of Art and the administrative expenses and costs of operation thereof."

The Senate and House Committees held hearings on the bill. Mr. Mellon arranged for a number of witnesses who could testify as to the importance and value of the Mellon Collection and the suitability of the site on the Mall. Lord Duveen came, as did Charles Henschel of Knoedler's; also John Russell Pope, the architect; and N. A. Townsend, representing the Department of Justice; Frederick A. Delano, representing the National Capital Park and Planning Commission; Charles Moore, Chairman, Commission of Fine Arts; Dr. Charles G. Abbot, Secretary, Smithsonian Institution; A. K. Shipe, attorney for the George Washington Memorial Association; Colonel Dan I. Sultan, Engineer Commissioner for the District of Columbia; Harry S. Wender, Chairman, Committee on Safety, Federation of Citizens Association; and Donald D. Shepard, trustee of The A. W. Mellon Educational and Charitable Trust. I also testified, giving a short history of the Collection and mentioning its scope and the quality of the paintings and sculpture.

The Committees reported House Joint Resolution 217 (Public Resolution No. 14, 75th Congress) to their respective Houses, with their approval. The bill went through the Senate and House of Representatives with practically no opposition. The National Gallery of Art had come into being with a charter from Congress, containing all the provisions which, Mr. Mellon felt, would safeguard the future of the institution.

The most important provisons are, first, that the National Gallery of Art, although a unit of the Smithsonian Institution, should be governed entirely by its own Board of Trustees; and second, that "The faith of the United States is pledged that . . . the United States will provide such funds as may be necessary for the upkeep of the National Gallery of Art and the Administrative expenses and costs of operation thereof;" also that "no work of art shall be included in the Permanent Collection of the National Gallery of Art unless it be of similar high standard of quality to those in the collection acquired from the donor."

Donald Shepard and I, who had watched the proceedings from

the gallery of the House of Representatives, went immediately from the Capitol to Mr. Mellon at 1785 Massachusetts Avenue, to tell him that the National Gallery was now an established fact, or would be as soon as President Roosevelt signed the bill, which he did on March 24, 1937.

Preparations were made to organize the National Gallery as soon as possible. At a special meeting of the Board of Regents of the Smithsonian Institution on June 24, 1937, the following general trustees of the National Gallery of Art were elected; Andrew W. Mellon, David K. E. Bruce, S. Parker Gilbert, Duncan Phillips, and Donald D. Shepard. The trustees ex officio at that time were the Chief Justice of the United States, Charles Evans Hughes; the Secretary of State, Cordell Hull; the Secretary of the Treasury, Henry Morgenthau, Jr.; and the Secretary of the Smithsonian Institution, Dr. Charles G. Abbot.

Mr. Mellon, in his offer to erect a building for the National Gallery, had stated that he would provide an endowment of $5,000,000, the income to be used to buy works of art and also to pay the salaries of the five executive staff officers, but not for the upkeep of the Gallery. This sum, later increased to $10,000,000, was donated by the trustees of The A. W. Mellon Educational and Charitable Trust. The income from this fund has enabled the Gallery to buy many works of art which have added greatly to its resources in the fields of painting and sculpture.

VIII

The Building Is Erected

Mr. Mellon had chosen John Russell Pope of New York as architect for the building of the National Gallery of Art. Mr. Pope, one of America's most distinguished architects, had had extensive experience in designing art museums. Mr. Mellon had been greatly impressed by Mr. Pope's work on the Archives Building, which had brought him in contact with Mr. Mellon.

Fortunately Mr. Pope lost no time in completing the design for the exterior of the National Gallery building and also made the plans for the interior, including air conditioning for the entire building. Mr. Mellon approved these plans and was satisfied that the building for the National Gallery would be beautiful and also practical in its operation, and as comfortable for the staff and visitors as possible in a building of this size.

Mr. Mellon had only a short time to live, though none of us knew this; and Mr. Pope, the architect of the Gallery, was to die within twenty-four hours after Mr. Mellon. The few remaining months were filled with discussions about the design of the Gallery, the acquisition of paintings; and many other things.

Mr. Mellon himself chose the marble for the exterior of the building. At the suggestion of Mr. Pope, Mr. Mellon and I had gone to New York and looked at two or three buildings with exterior walls of "Tennessee pink marble" which comes in varying shades of pink to white. Each piece must be quarried and matched, for in wet weather the marble turns a slightly pink color and in the sunshine it absorbs the light, rather than reflects it as so many other marbles do.

All this involved a certain amount of waste, which made an undertaking of this magnitude very expensive. At a later meeting in Washington with the architect and several others, including Paul Mellon, David Bruce, and Donald Shepard, trustees of The A. W. Mellon Educational and Charitable Trust, Mr. Andrew Mellon was told that the Tennessee marble would cost a great deal more than any other. "That is not important," said Mr. Mellon. "It is by far the most beautiful and it will last, I hope, a long time, so use it." That is the kind of decision which only the donor can make so quickly. It was the kind of thing that would involve endless wrangles of expediency among committees and trustees who must share responsibility for such decisions. In order to secure the marble needed, James Stuart and Alexander Reed, who had been retained by the Mellon trustees to represent them in technical matters such as this, went to Tennessee and did a most excellent job in securing marble, properly matched, from the only sources available. Mr. Stuart and Mr. Reed were also invaluable in working out, with the architect and with the Building Committee, consisting of Harry McBride, John Walker, and myself, plans for securing and installing material for the interior of the building, also for colors in the various rooms. These recommendations were always submitted to the Mellon trustees for their comments and approval.

Mr. Pope's design was inspired by the old Court House building in Washington, designed by George Hadfield and built about 1820 in Judiciary Square. Mr. Pope and I sat in front of it for hours. He explained to me how he intended to design a building in the form of a double-H. surmounted by a low dome, with columns and pediments on each end as well as on the two sides. Mr. Mellon was not happy about the multitude of columns. I suggested that we talk with Mr. Pope about it. "Mr. Pope is a very high-powered man," said Mr. Mellon, "I would not want to hurt his feelings." "I know Mr. Pope very well," I said. "Let me talk with him." "Go ahead," said Mr. Mellon, "and see what you can do."

Mr. Pope was always amenable to suggestions, if he thought they had merit. I explained that, in Mr. Mellon's and my opinion as laymen, it was enough to have a pediment and columns in the center of the north and south sides of the building but that a pediment and columns on the east and west ends would distract the eye from the central motif and make for restlessness. Mr. Pope said he thought that might well be the case and he would study the design and come back to us. He did so, with the beautiful blank walls and the large doors on the east and west sides of the building, and the setbacks on the roof which hide the glass skylights that otherwise would have glittered in the sun. He was delighted with the change and so was Mr. Mellon.

That was almost the last active part Mr. Mellon was able to take, so far as the Gallery was concerned. He had long before given to The A. W. Mellon Educational and Charitable Trust securities more than adequate to meet all the Gallery's requirements. He had the utmost confidence in the trustees he had placed in charge of the Trust; his son, Paul Mellon; his son-in-law, David Bruce; and his personal attorney, Donald Shepard. His confidence was more than justified. These three men devoted themselves to carrying out Mr. Mellon's wishes, exercising rare judgment in deciding many difficult questions that would arise.

Excavations for the foundation of the building had been started by July. The weather was getting very hot and Mr. Mellon was showing exhaustion for the first time. It was arranged that he would go to the house of his daughter, Mrs. Bruce, at Southampton, Long Island, and a private railroad car was engaged to take him from Washington through New York City to Long Island. As he drove down Pennsylvania Avenue to the Union Station, he saw the site for the National Gallery for the last time and was happy to see that the work had started. He died in Southampton on August 26, 1937.

Mr. Pope died at Newport the next night. My wife and I went to Mr. Mellon's funeral in Pittsburgh. There I rode to the cemetery in the car with Ogden Mills and Parker Gilbert, both devoted friends of Mr. Mellon, and both were to die within the year. From there my wife and I went to Mr. Pope's funeral in Newport.

It was with a devastating sense of loss that we returned to Washington. Mr. Mellon's work was taken up by Paul Mellon, David Bruce, and Donald Shepard, and carried to a triumphant conclusion, as may be seen in the Gallery today. John Russell Pope was succeeded by his associates, Otto Eggers and Daniel Higgins. Mr. Eggers had the responsibility for completing the design of the building for the National Gallery; and, with his fine sense of proportion and great knowledge of architecture, carried the work to a most successful end. Mr. Higgins did a tremendous job in organizing the work, and other members of the architectural staff, such as T. J. Young, also made important contributions. We also had access to advice from William Adams Delano, an architect of great knowledge and taste. Lammot Belin, when he joined the Board of Trustees, made many valuable suggestions about the interior of the building and particularly about the garden courts.

When Mr. Pope died, the design for the interior of the building had been largely settled. It had been decided, during the lifetime of Mr. Mellon and Mr. Pope, that there would be a rotunda, as now, also two garden courts and two sculpture halls surrounded by exhibition galleries as may be seen at present. But no decision had been reached on questions such as the material to compose the great columns in the rotunda—whether they should be of green marble or limestone. This was the subject of the last talk I had with Mr. Pope, when my wife and I were staying with Mr. and Mrs. Pope in Newport, shortly before his death. He rather favored green marble; but before a conclusion was reached after his death, Mr. Eggers brought to Washington small sample columns of all the material under consideration. The trustees of the Mellon Trust settled on the dark green marble which could be acquired from a quarry near Lucca in Italy. Here again Mr. Stuart and Mr. Reed were most helpful in going to Italy and making the necessary arrangements for securing the marble.

Each column was composed of five marble drums, and they were raised into place through an opening in the floor where the fountain now is. They were immediately sheathed in wood, to protect them from dust. Finally Mr. Eggers told me that all the columns were in place, that the wooden sheaths had been removed, and that we could

Rotunda of the National Gallery of Art

see the effect. I shall never forget the nervousness with which I entered the rotunda. If the columns were wrong, nothing could ever be done about it. But they were not wrong; and they stand there now supporting the dome and seem perfect for this purpose.

The architects had proposed green tiles as the covering for the interior of the dome. All of us felt that green tiles would not be the solution. John Walker, who was to be Chief Curator and later my successor as Director, had come from Rome for a week or two, to study the Kress Collection of paintings and sculpture which Mr. Samuel Kress had decided to give to the National Gallery. John Walker suggested a coffered ceiling of plaster similar in design to the one in the Pantheon in Rome; and that suggestion was followed with great success.

Mr. Eggers designed the fountain in the rotunda, placing at its apex the bronze figure of Mercury attributed to Adriaen de Vries in the Mellon Collection. That was done, also with great success. William Adams Delano, the well-known architect, was going through the Gallery with me one day. "The placing of the *Mercury* is perfect," he said. "If it had been any larger, it would have been too small. It would have been too assertive, as if trying to fill such a vast space. As it is, it is like a jewel on a woman's dress. It is beautiful but keeps to scale."

The marble floors in the rotunda and the sculpture halls proved very difficult. The architects furnished only designs that were far too "busy." Finally, I went to Irwin Laughlin, a friend of Mr. Mellon and of mine, who was very knowledgeable about architecture and decoration. He climbed a ladder in his library, got down some books on design of French garden parterres; and worked out with me the floor designs that can now be seen in the rotunda and the two sculpture halls.

Mr. Laughlin was also most helpful in choosing colors for the painted panelled walls in the Gallery's English, French, and American rooms. In his own beautiful Meridian House in Washington, he had followed the French technique of painting the walls, first with orange or vermillion, then six coats of green or white paint, using in each case different shades of green or white for the panels and for the moldings. This we did in the panelled rooms at The Gallery, matching colors on the walls of Mr. Laughlin's house. It is this variation in shades of the same color that gives the rooms their subtle but lively coloring.

Before Mr. Mellon's death, he had talked with me about the decoration of the exhibition rooms on the main floor of the Gallery. He wanted the rooms to be harmonious settings for the paintings and sculpture, but not too elaborate. I suggested that the rooms give some indication of the place and period that had produced the works of art but that they should not be old period rooms. I recommended painted plaster for the walls and travertine stone for the doorways and trim of the rooms in which Italian paintings were shown up to the period of Titian and Tintoretto; after that, damask covered walls with travertine trim. For the Rembrandts and other Dutch paintings, I suggested oak panelling of not too dark a color; and in the East Wing of the building, painted panelling, with French, English, or American overdoors and cornices. Mr. Mellon was delighted with these suggestions. I warned that they would prove expensive. "I don't care how expensive they are," said Mr. Mellon, "if they don't look expensive."

That remark was typical of Mr. Mellon's innate good taste. It was also of the greatest help to me when the architects later tried to gild the lily by too much carving in the Rembrandt rooms. On the other hand, I told them, with the approval of the Mellon trustees, to do as they liked in the van Dyck rooms, where the architects produced the rather grand but beautiful setting in which the van Dycks in the Mellon, Widener, and Kress Collections now hang.

David Bruce suggested the panelling in the Founders Room, off the rotunda. It made a handsome setting for the portraits which have been placed there, and also a comfortable and sympathetic room for visitors who wished to read and smoke and relax after making a tour of the Gallery.

When Mr. Mellon died, he knew and we knew of no other works of art that were coming to the National Gallery. So at first the architects made plans to hang the Mellon paintings in the two large sculpture halls, surrounded by a series of square or oblong rooms, with ceilings twenty-five feet high. When I saw the drawings, I realized that such arrangements would not be satisfactory, especially as the Kress Collection and the Widener Collection might some day come to the National Gallery.

All museum directors who know their collections must guide the architects in designing the size and shape of the rooms where the works of art are to be shown. The trustees of the Mellon Trust had given me authority in such details, subject always to their approval. So I told Mr. Eggers, in confidence, that the Kress Collection was coming to the National Gallery and that we hoped the Widener Collection would also come, although nothing could be said publicly at that time. I told Mr. Eggers that the two long sculpture halls were to be used as settings for large sculpture; that the West Hall would contain the bronze statues, representing *Venus* and *Bacchus,* by Sansovino in the Mellon Collection, and the East Hall the two marble urns by Clodion, also in the Mellon Collection; and that the paintings would be distributed in the rooms opening off these two sculpture halls and around the two garden courts.

Next I made, with my wife's assistance, a rough sketch for a floor plan with rooms of varying sizes, placing the doors in such a way that one could see through them a painting or a piece of sculpture, not another door or a series of doors as in so many other galleries. At intervals we placed small octagonal rooms for the Renaissance sculpture, such as Room No. 2 in which the painted terra-cotta sculpture by Donatello is now shown; and Room No. 6 in which the marble sculpture by Desiderio da Settignano, Laurana, and others can be seen. We also made a sketch of a plan for the round room in which Mr. Widener's *David* by Donatello could be placed; for the octagonal room in which the painted wood sculpture by Nino Pisano in the Kress Collection is now installed and for the connecting corridor which is now a setting for Mr. Kress' small marble angels and plaques.

Mr. Eggers, with his great sense of proportion and knowledge of

East Garden Court of the National Gallery of Art

architecture, took these rough sketches and made them into professional architectural plans and renderings, which were carried out with the approval of the Mellon trustees. On the south side of the Gallery, opening off the West Garden Court, a sketch for an octagonal room for sculpture was made by Charles Seymour, Jr., the Curator of Sculpture. It was intended to show certain Gothic sculpture which, sad to relate, never came to Washington. A round room was designed, opening off the East Garden Court, which now provides a setting for works by Houdon. By this time we knew that the Kress Collection would come to the National Gallery and we hoped the

Widener Collection would also, though it was uncertain as to the date when the Widener Collection might come.

The two garden courts Mr. Eggers designed with the court in the Frick Collection in New York in mind. At William Adams Delano's suggestion, the beds were filled, not with earth, but with pebbles on which the tubs with growing plants could be placed. Later, in Palm Beach, I saw the graceful "fishtail" palms growing in tubs, even in badly lighted interiors. The Mellon trustees agreed to buy enough to decorate both garden courts, and the plants arrived at the Gallery, rolled up like umbrellas. In the early years of the Gallery blooming flowers in pots were bought from greenhouses for decoration of the garden courts and around the fountain in the rotunda. Now the Gallery has its own greenhouses, built inside the moat walls, and a highly competent horticulturist, Noel Smith, has been in charge, to my great satisfaction, since the Gallery was first opened.

The architect, Mr. Eggers, had designed a central fountain for each of the two garden courts. The fountains needed handsome sculpture to relieve their severity. I cabled Irwin Laughlin, who was then in Paris, asking him to try to find suitable sculpture for these fountains. He went to his favorite dealer, who told him that he had sent two lead fountains to the New York World's Fair, where they could be seen, Mr. Laughlin said, outside the French Pavilion. John Walker and I went at once to New York to see them. They were perfect for our purpose—small lead fountains with figures by Tubi and Legros. They had stood in the park at Versailles as background for a little theater. The trustees of the Mellon Trust were equally enthusiastic and bought the two fountains for the garden courts, where they now stand.

There remained the question of the height of the exhibition galleries. Mr. Eggers proposed twenty-five feet; we finally compromised on twenty-one. Before the work was completed Joseph Widener had decided that the great collection, which he and his father had brought together, should come to Washington. The question had been settled; Mr. Widener had come to the National Gallery to inspect the rooms where his paintings and sculpture and other works of art would be shown. He mentioned that the cornices should be a little deeper and I agreed. I thought he was right but I would have agreed anyhow at that stage of events! That night he went to his racing farm near Lexington, Kentucky. Next day he called me on long distance. "I have been thinking about things since I left you and I have changed my mind." "Yes," I said, fearing the worst, "what is it?" "I thought those cornices ought to be a little deeper—say six inches." "You couldn't be more right," I said, heaving a sigh of relief. "Would you like them to be twelve inches deeper?"

In order to avoid mistakes, the architects made, at the request of the Mellon trustees, a model of the exterior of the building and also one of the interior.

The building of the National Gallery aroused great interest, not only in Washington, but throughout the country. Many persons came to see it and expressed admiration for its style and harmony, and for its spaciousness that provided for expansion in rooms not then open to view. At the same time it gave the works of art a setting of intimacy, or at least one that was in scale with the works themselves.

One day I had a telephone call from Justice Harlan Stone, who was a friend of Mr. Mellon's and also of mine and was afterwards to become Chief Justice of the United States and thereby ex officio Chairman of our Board of Trustees. He had a deep interest in art and was very knowledgeable about paintings. "Mrs. Stone and I are longing to see the National Gallery. Could we come soon?" I said, "Of course, come this afternoon if you can." They started on a tour of the rooms, rather depressed; soon they brightened and broke into enthusiastic comments about everything. "We were afraid to come," they said. "We knew Mr. Mellon had left plenty of money and we were terrified that the Gallery would be overdone. But it is perfect and we couldn't be happier!"

Another day we had a visit from a famous lady with great taste. She liked everything about the Gallery, especially "those beautiful bare walls. Couldn't you keep them this way and not clutter them with pictures?"

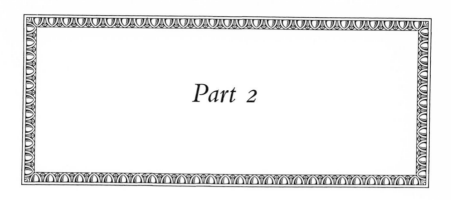

Part 2

IX

The National Gallery Is Organized

At a meeting on March 9, 1938, the three surviving general trustees elected Paul Mellon to serve the unexpired term of his father, the late Andrew W. Mellon, and Ferdinand Lammot Belin to serve the unexpired term of the late S. Parker Gilbert, who had died on February 23, 1938.

On March 9, 1938, an organization meeting of the trustees of the National Gallery of Art was held in the Regents' Room of the Smithsonian Institution; and a draft of bylaws was adopted as the bylaws of the National Gallery. The bylaws provide that the executive officers shall consist of the chairman of the Board of Trustees, who shall be the Chief Justice of the United States, trustee ex officio, also the president of the Board, the vice president, secretary, treasurer, director, administrator, chief curator, and assistant director.

The following officers were elected: Paul Mellon, President; David K. E. Bruce, Vice President; Donald D. Shepard, Secretary and Treasurer; and David E. Finley, Director. An Executive Committee was authorized, consisting of five trustees; an Acquisitions Committee, consisting of four trustees and the Director; and a Finance Committee, consisting of five trustees.

On May 26, 1939, the general trustees elected Joseph E. Widener of Philadelphia to fill the vacancy on the Board occasioned by the resignation of Paul Mellon. They also elected Samuel H. Kress of New York to fill the vacancy caused by the resignation of Donald D. Shepard, as a trustee. Mr. Shepard continued to serve as Secretary-Treasurer and General Counsel. At this meeting, David Bruce was elected President, and Lammot Belin, Vice President. Stephen Pichetto of New York was appointed Consultant Restorer of Paintings.

The National Gallery had great luck in finding the right staff. John Walker, the Chief Curator, had gone from Pittsburgh to Harvard and then to Florence to be an assistant to Bernard Berenson at I Tatti. There he acquired a wide and scholarly knowledge of art and particularly of Western painting and sculpture. Later he had become a member of the staff of The American Academy in Rome; and while he was there he had the good fortune to marry Lady Margaret Drummond, the charming and intelligent daughter of the British Ambassador to Italy. John Walker was appointed Chief Curator at a meeting of the Board of Trustees on August 31, 1938, and reported for duty on January 1, 1939. Then began a happy association for me which lasted during all the years I was Director of the Gallery and afterwards. We happened to have the same taste in paintings and sculpture; and with John Walker, as with the others on the staff, there was none of the intramural unhappiness that mars life in so many museums. He was also of the greatest assistance in working with the Mellon trustees and with the architect and with Mr. Stuart and Mr. Reed and with me in determining the architectural arrangements and securing the materials for the interior of the building.

Charles Seymour, Jr., was appointed Curator of Sculpture and a very scholarly one he was, with great taste as well as knowledge. I always urged our curators to be completely honest and independent in their judgment and in their attributions of works of art. Both the trustees and I upheld them, even when it involved an attribution to a less celebrated artist than had been the case heretofore. After all, that is part of the business of a museum—to adhere to the truth insofar as the truth can be known.

Harry McBride was appointed, on August 31, 1938, Administrator in charge of the building, its personnel, and innumerable other things. He and his wife had served with distinction in our foreign service. Harry McBride had a splendid grasp of what was required in the operation of the building and of the persons to operate it, and how to choose them from the Civil Service list. He also knew about printing and publications and was of great help in finding competent publishers and in securing accurate color reproductions of paintings in the National Gallery for books which were published by the Gallery and sold in the Publications Rooms, together with excellent color postcards. With Harry McBride's help, plans were worked out for a small auditorium and for a cafeteria to be operated by Government Services, Inc. It was due to him, also, that a small dining room was provided for the staff and one for the Director and any guests he might have; also more offices for the staff and additional storage space of which no museum can have enough.

Harry McBride assembled an able staff for the administration of the building, including George T. Heckert, Charles B. Walstrom, and Joseph Brearton. An outstanding member of Harry McBride's staff was Sterling Eagleton, who was Chief Engineer and Building Superintendent. Mr. Eagleton did valuable research in the fields of temperature and humidity control and in lighting; also in devising measures for the security of the Gallery's collection.

Macgill James, former Director of the Peale Museum in Baltimore, joined the staff as Assistant Director in 1940. He not only brought his knowledge of museums but "humanized" the Gallery in many ways. He made visitors to the Gallery feel welcome, especially people from other museums, many of whom he knew. His wife, Bruce Kinsolving James, was a person of great distinction; and after her death, Macgill married another charming lady, Caroline Rogers, who was of great help to Macgill and to all of us in making the Gallery a cheerful, hospitable place.

In 1943, Huntington Cairns was elected by the trustees as Secretary-Treasurer and General Counsel of the Gallery to take the place of Donald D. Shepard, resigned. Mr. Cairns brought to the National Gallery not only his extensive knowledge of the law but also a wide-ranging scholarship in the visual arts and literature, which added greatly to the prestige of the Gallery.

Without these five men—John Walker, Harry McBride, Charles Seymour, Jr., Huntington Cairns, and Macgill James, the Gallery and its collections could never have developed as they did. Later, during my years as Director, the Gallery benefitted by the scholarly contributions of Charles Parkhurst, Perry Cott, Lester Cooke, William Adams, Fern Shapley, and others. I shall always be grateful to them and to Ernest Feidler, James Adams, and the other members of our remarkable and devoted staff at the National Gallery.

I must mention, too, my own secretaries. A man's career can often be handicapped if there is not courtesy and efficiency on the part of those who run his office. I was very fortunate in having as secretaries in the beginning Miss Marie Ray and Miss Phyllis Roos; and later Miss Susan Bennett and Mrs. Elizabeth Foy.

In all these years, Miss Bennett has shown intelligence and devotion to her work and, after her retirement from Government service, has been of the greatest assistance to me in locating and verifying many of the facts cited in this book.

All those whose names appear in this book and others not specifically mentioned helped to make the National Gallery what it is today; and futhermore, I think they enjoyed doing it, as I did.

As I write these lines, changes have come to the Gallery, as are inevitable in all institutions. John Walker has retired, after a most distinguished career as Chief Curator and later as Director of the National Gallery. The trustees have elected as the next Director, John Carter Brown, who has served as Assistant Director and has shown that he has the ability, the knowledge, and the personality to carry the National Gallery to even greater heights, as I am sure he will do.

X

Policy of the National Gallery

At an early meeting of the Board of Trustees soon after the Gallery was established, a statement of policy was approved governing the acquisition and exhibition of works of art in the National Gallery.

First of all, the trustees recognized that the policy governing the acquisition of works of art for the Gallery must conform to the provisions of Section 5 of the Joint Resolution of the Congress establishing the National Gallery, which specify that "no work of art shall be included in the Permanent Collection of the National Gallery of Art unless it be of similar high standard of quality to those in the Collection acquired from the donor"—(Andrew W. Mellon). This standard of quality has been faithfully adhered to by the trustees and staff of the Gallery, so that its collections are conspicuous for their extraordinary and uniformly high quality.

It was also provided that no work of art shall be acquired by purchase, gift, bequest, or otherwise, unless with the approval of the Board of Trustees upon recommendation of the Acquisitions Committee.

Works of art acquired for the Gallery shall become part of and be exhibited with the Permanent Collection or be stored in the Gallery or exhibited in rooms on the ground floor.

Important exhibitions may be held but, except with the approval of the Board of Trustees, no objects in the Permanent Collection shall be loaned for exhibition outside the Gallery until the collection has been greatly augmented. This made it possible to avoid the embarrassment of lending works of art to one museum and refusing to do so to others. Later, an exception was made in the case of American paintings because it was thought that a retrospective exhibition of the work of an American artist should show his or her best works, including those in the National Gallery.

The policy adopted states that the Permanent Collection shall, with rare exceptions, include only paintings, sculpture, and the graphic arts, representative of the schools of American and European art and their sources. Exceptions shall be made only when the Gallery acquires, by gift or bequest, a collection which includes other objects in addition to paintings, sculpture, and the graphic arts. This provision made it possible to accept the Widener Collection with its Chinese porcelains and crystals and other rare and beautiful objects.

Another provision was that the Permanent Collection shall include only such paintings, sculpture, and examples of the graphic arts as are representative of artists whose merit and importance have been generally recognized for twenty years following their death. The Gallery may acquire works by artists who have been dead less than twenty years but these works must not be shown with the Permanent Collection until they are eligible to become part of that collection.

This is the usual provision in national galleries, such as those in London and Paris. It not only protects the trustees and staff, who are not infallible, but it also protects the public and the taxpayers from indefinite responsibility for the care of objects which have not proved their worth.

Last and one of the most important provisions was that no gifts or bequests of works of art shall be accepted subject to restrictions as to their being permanently segregated or exhibited as a collection; but any gift accepted shall be exhibited with the Permanent Collection or with more recent ones on the ground floor, or stored as may be deemed most appropriate by the Acquisitions Committee. This provision, adhered to in all cases, has saved the visitor to the National Gallery the confusion that arises from collections shown as units.

The National Gallery was able to attract other works of art, first, because Mr. Mellon had provided a beautiful building and his great collection as a standard of quality for the new museum, and, second, because he had minimized his own contribution as much as possible. He stipulated that the gallery should not bear his name and he wished also that his paintings and sculpture should not be shown as a unit but should be mingled with the other works of art which he hoped would come to the new museum.

Although Mr. Mellon wanted and expected no special recognition of all that he had done, it was inevitable that it would come, as it did, in actions by the National Gallery trustees, by friends, and by the United States Government.

There is, of course, a portrait of Mr. Mellon in the Founders Room off the rotunda, along with portraits of other important donors. And after Mr. Mellon's death, the trustees erected in the Constitution Avenue entrance to the Gallery a memorial tablet, with an inscription giving the dates of Mr. Mellon's birth and death, 1855-1937. There is a profile portrait of Mr. Mellon in marble by the well-known sculptor, Walker Hancock. There is also a quotation from the oration by Pericles over the dead in the Peloponnesian War:

For the whole earth is the sepulchre of famous men; and their story is not graven only on stone over their native earth, but lives on far away, without visible symbol, woven into the stuff of other men's lives.

Later, a beautiful fountain was erected in memory of Mr. Mellon in the small triangular park at the intersection of Pennsylvania and Constitution Avenues at Sixth Street, directly facing the National Gallery's north entrance. The money was raised by private subscriptions, contributed by friends. Authorization to erect the fountain at this site was granted to the Andrew W. Mellon Memorial Committee by a Joint Resolution of the Senate and House of Representatives, approved July 16, 1947. At the dedication ceremony on May 9, 1952, the fountain was assigned to the Secretary of the Interior for operation by the National Park Service.

The fountain, which was designed by the architect, Otto R. Eggers, is in the shape of a large bronze bowl, decorated by the sculptor, Sidney Waugh, with twelve sculptural signs of the zodiac, in high bronze relief, applied to the wall of the lowest bronze basin. The fountain is a handsome addition to the city's ornaments and is appropriate to the climate of Washington, which cannot have too many fountains.

In recognition of Mr. Mellon's services to the nation, the United States Government, through its Post Office Department, in December 1955, issued a three-cent stamp bearing the portrait of Andrew W. Mellon. It was issued during the centennial year of Mr. Mellon's birth and a commemorative ceremony was held in the auditorium of the National Gallery at noon on December 20th, inaugurating the first-day issue of the stamp.

Postmaster General Arthur E. Summerfield and United States Senator Edward Martin of Pennsylvania were the principal speakers and a response, on behalf of the Mellon family, was made by Mr. Mellon's son, Paul Mellon.

As Mr. Mellon anticipated, the prestige of the National Gallery was increased from the very beginning by the distinguished men who became general trustees and trustees ex officio. At the time this book was written, five men had served successively as Chairman of the Board of Trustees; Chief Justices of the United States Charles Evans Hughes, Harlan Fiske Stone, Fred M. Vinson, Earl Warren, and Warren E. Burger.

There have been nine Secretaries of State: Cordell Hull, E. R. Stettinius, James F. Byrnes, George C. Marshall, Dean Acheson, John Foster Dulles, Christian Herter, Dean Rusk, and William P. Rogers.

Ten Secretaries of the Treasury have served on the Board: Henry Morgenthau, Jr., Fred M. Vinson, John W. Snyder, George M. Humphrey, Robert B. Anderson, C. Douglas Dillon, Henry Fowler, David M. Kennedy, John B. Connally, and George P. Shultz.

Four Secretaries of the Smithsonian Institution have been ex officio members of the Board of Trustees of the National Gallery: Charles G. Abbot, Alexander Wetmore, Leonard Carmichael, and S. Dillon Ripley.

In addition to the four ex officio trustees, the Board now includes Paul Mellon, President; Franklin Murphy; Lessing J. Rosenwald; Stoddard Stevens; and John Hay Whitney.

Others who have served as general trustees are: Ferdinand Lammot Belin, David K. E. Bruce, Chester Dale, S. Parker Gilbert, John N. Irwin II, Samuel H. Kress, Rush H. Kress, Andrew W. Mellon, Duncan Phillips, Donald D. Shepard, and Joseph E. Widener.

The judgment and experience of these distinguished men have been of invaluable aid in the development of the National Gallery.

XI

The Kress Collection

It was very important that, when the Gallery should be first opened to the public, it should contain at least a few works of art other than those given by Mr. Mellon, and thus be on the way, as he wished, toward becoming a joint undertaking on the part of the federal government and private collectors who desired to form a great National Gallery in Washington.

This, happily, was made possible by Samuel H. Kress of New York and the Samuel H. Kress Foundation. Mr. Kress, who had created, by his own ability and with his own savings, a great mercantile establishment, had become interested in art and had collected a large number of paintings and sculptures, all of the Italian school. His collection had by this time reached a point where he felt he must make some provision for its future. He was considering building and endowing a museum of Italian art in New York, and, I was told, had even secured an option on some land on upper Fifth Avenue.

I had met Mr. Kress on the *Bremen* when my wife and I were crossing to Europe in 1936. He mentioned very modestly that he had "a few pictures" and at my request said he would be glad to show them to me when we returned to America. I made two or three attempts to see him in New York during the following months; but each time he was sick or out of town and said he would like to show me his collection himself.

Meanwhile help came from another source. Jeremiah O'Connor, then Curator at the Corcoran Gallery of Art, and Dr. Herbert Friedmann, Curator at the Smithsonian Institution, had visited the Kress Collection in January 1938 and were amazed at the fine paintings and sculpture they had seen. On returning to Washington, Mr. O'Connor wrote to Mr. Kress urging that he give his collection to the National Gallery which had by this time been established, with its building well under way. Mr. Kress was interested, at least to the extent of talking with me; and when Mr. O'Connor transmitted the invitation to me, I went at once to New York.

I was deeply impressed with the scope and the high quality of Mr. Kress' collection. It covered the entire Italian School from the thirteenth to the eighteenth centuries and with the paintings and sculpture in Mr. Mellon's collection and those coming, we hoped, from Mr. Widener, would at once make the National Gallery one of the outstanding museums in the field of Italian art.

I arrived at Mr. Kress' apartment at 1020 Fifth Avenue at three o'clock on April 22, 1938. We looked at his paintings and talked all afternoon. He asked me to stay on to dinner, which I did; and when I finally left in time to take the midnight train back to Washington Mr. Kress had decided to give his collection to the National Gallery. "And I will give it to you," he said, "in time for the opening of the Gallery." "Also," he said, "as I can obtain other works of art, I will exchange them for some of those I am giving you now." He had, for instance, six paintings by Sano di Pietro. Later, he and, afterwards, his brother Rush Kress exchanged five of these paintings for others which were needed to fill out the collection.

At first, Mr. Kress had expressed the wish that his collection be shown as a unit. It was a natural desire. He had never married and he looked upon his collection as something that would represent him in all the years ahead. I told him of Mr. Mellon's desire that no collections should be shown as a unit; that he wanted the works of art, given by others, as well as himself, to be shown either by schools or chronologically, as might be most intelligible and enjoyable to visitors to the Gallery. I also told him that, as he had only Italian paintings and sculpture, they could be shown in rooms containing only his own gifts; but that the Florentine rooms would be contiguous to the rooms containing Mr. Mellon's Florentine paintings, his Venetian rooms next to other Venetian rooms, and the same arrangement made for his Sienese and north Italian paintings. Mr.

Kress was quite happy with this plan, for he wanted the public to get the utmost enjoyment from his collection.

The trustees of the Gallery approved all these arrangements, which were afterwards carried out. First of all, it was necessary, in agreement with Mr. Kress, to select the paintings and the sculpture which were to come to the National Gallery. I cabled John Walker, who was to be Chief Curator and was then with the American Academy in Rome, asking him to meet me in New York in order to consult with Mr. Kress as to the works that would be included in his great donation to the Gallery. John arrived shortly after Christmas 1938 and we spent together some time with Mr. Kress and some time alone, studying everything in his apartment and in the Kress offices downtown, where many of his paintings were kept. At last we had a list of three hundred and seventy-five paintings and sixteen pieces of sculpture, all of the Italian School, which Mr. Kress agreed to give to the National Gallery. Photographs were supplied for the use of members of the Acquisitions Committee. They were, of course, delighted to approve Mr. Kress' generous offer and to recommend it to the trustees who promptly accepted it.

I said to Mr. Kress as John Walker and I were leaving on that day in Christmas week 1938: "We are taking *all* the paintings in your apartment. It is going to be very bare and I feel rather badly about it." "Don't worry," he said, "I shall get along all right, and I am glad to know my paintings will be enjoyed by so many people."

I grew very fond of Mr. Kress. He was a strong character, very definite but very fair, and he developed a great devotion to the National Gallery, and a desire to make his collection and thus the Gallery as distinguished as possible.

He had succeeded in bringing together one of the most complete collections of Italian paintings and sculpture ever assembled by one man. It included such early works as *The Calling of Peter and Andrew*, painted by Duccio in 1308-1311; the *Madonna and Child* by Giotto, painted circa 1320; and Domenico Veneziano's *Saint John in the Desert*. There were paintings by Simone Martini, Gentile da Fabriano, Masolino, Fra Angelico, Filippo, and Filippino Lippi, Piero di

Giorgione, The Adoration of the Shepherds, *Samuel H. Kress Collection*

Cosimo, Sassetta, and Giovanni di Paolo, There were also fine examples of the work of Ghirlandaio, Signorelli, Andrea del Sarto, Perugino, Mantegna, Correggio, and Crivelli. There was a small room of frescoes, painted by Luini about 1507 for a house near Milan, which had been transferred to canvas and were installed in a room in the National Gallery. One of the most beautiful and important paintings acquired by Mr. Kress was *The Adoration of the Shepherds* by Giorgione. The Collection also contained well-known paintings by Raphael, Titian, Lotto, Carpaccio, Giovanni Bellini, Tintoretto, and Tiepolo. And there were North Italian paintings by Cossa, Tura, Dosso Dossi, and Ercole Roberti, such as are seldom seen in this

Fra Angelico and Fra Filippo Lippi, The Adoration of the Magi,
Samuel H. Kress Collection

country. Equally remarkable was the Italian sculpture which the
Kress Collection brought to the National Gallery, including dis-
tinguished works by Lorenzo Ghiberti, Jacopo della Quercia,
Desiderio da Settignano, Antonio Rossellino, Donatello, Mino da
Fiesole, Verrocchio, Giovanni della Robbia, Benedetto da Maiano,
and Amadeo.

Giotto, Madonna and Child, *Samuel H. Kress Collection*

Antonio Rossellino, The Young Saint John the Baptist, *Samuel H. Kress Collection*

François Clouet, "Diane de Poitiers," *Samuel H. Kress Collection*

Mr. Kress was a trustee and President of the National Gallery for many years. Toward the end he could not come to the meetings and John Walker and I, and others of the staff, would go to his apartment in New York from time to time and talk with him about the Gallery. His eyes would brighten as we mentioned his paintings and the pleasure they gave to visitors. Mr. Kress died in September 1955. His brother, Rush H. Kress, succeeded him as Chairman of the Samuel H. Kress Foundation and as a trustee of the National Gallery.

Rush Kress was devoted to his brother, and his great ambition was to carry out Samuel H. Kress' wishes about the Kress Collection and the National Gallery. He kept around him the staff which his brother assembled for the work of the Foundation: Herbert Spencer; Guy Emerson; Miss Mary Davis; the art historian, Dr. William Suida; and the Restorer of Paintings, Stephen Pichetto, who was succeeded after his death by Mario Modestini. And a most able, resourceful and dedicated group they were.

Samuel Kress, long before he died, had broadened the scope of his collection. During the Christmas holidays of 1942, when he was at Hot Springs, Virginia, he telephoned, asking me to come there for a talk about matters that were bothering him. "I would like to build up my collection at the National Gallery," he said, "but there are no Italian paintings on the market that I want. Have you any suggestions?" "Yes," I said, "I do have a suggestion. The war has made it difficult to buy Italian paintings, but there is a very important collection of French paintings that has just come on the market in New York. And there is nothing the Gallery needs so much as French paintings of the seventeenth and eighteenth centuries."

Mr. Kress said he would like to see the French paintings and very soon he bought a distinguished group which included beautiful paintings by Chardin, Poussin, Louis LeNain, Fragonard, Drouais, Boucher, Greuze, and others. They completely filled two rooms in the East Wing of the Gallery and were harbingers of more to come. They were given in memory of Mr. Kress' brother, the late Claude Kress.

With this precedent, as indicating Samuel Kress' wishes, Rush Kress and his assistants proceeded to buy more paintings of the French

School, such as the full-length portrait *Napoleon in His Study* by Jacques-Louis David, and paintings by Chardin, Poussin, Claude Lorrain, and Ingres. One of the most important of all was the signed painting by Clouet, said to be a portrait of *"Diane de Poitiers"*; and there were also two rare fifteenth-century paintings by the "Master of Saint Gilles."

One day Rush Kress said to me: "I would like to get enough of the finest German paintings to fill at least one room." "It will be difficult," I said, "but there is nothing the Gallery needs more." So Mr. Kress and his staff got to work and as a result the National Gallery has a room completely filled with fine examples of the work of Holbein, Dürer, Altdorfer, Hans Baldung Grien, Strigel, and *The Small Crucifixion* by Grünewald.

This last picture gave me great satisfaction. John Walker had been in correspondence with Ernst Buschbeck, Director of the Kunsthistorisches Museum at Vienna with reference to the famous painting, *The Small Crucifixion,* by Grünewald. Dr. Buschbeck wanted the painting for his museum at Vienna. Finding that he could not acquire the painting for his museum, he wrote to John Walker to go ahead and buy the painting from its owner in The Netherlands for the National Gallery at Washington.

Mr. Kress was in Tucson, Arizona, with his family. I got a photograph of the painting and took the first train to Tucson. I liked to go there. Mr. Kress and his beautiful and charming wife, Virginia, were very kind to me and I enjoyed being with them.

Mr. Kress looked at the photograph of the Grünewald. I told him the price, which was quite high. He said yes, he would buy the painting and so it became a part of the Kress room of German paintings and one of the rarest and most important works in the Gallery.

Rush Kress continued to broaden the scope of the Kress Collection by acquiring Flemish, Spanish, and Dutch paintings as well as Italian paintings and sculpture.

The Flemish paintings included the beautiful *Presentation in the Temple* by Hans Memling; and Hieronymus Bosch's *Death and the Miser;* also two paintings by Peter Paul Rubens, which were greatly needed by the Gallery; and a painting by van Dyck.

Particularly important were the Spanish paintings, including the

Albrecht Dürer, Madonna and Child, *Samuel H. Kress Collection*

87

Mathis Grünewald, The Small Crucifixion, *Samuel H. Kress Collection*

famous *Laocoön* by El Greco, as well as other paintings by this great artist. During World War II, we had been asked to store the *Laocoön* at the National Gallery, which we were glad to do. We wanted very much to acquire the painting for the Gallery, and the owner eventually agreed to sell it. Mr. Kress and the Samuel H. Kress Foundation bought the painting; and it was hung as one of the newly acquired Kress paintings at the special Kress opening in 1946.

Rush Kress and the Kress Foundation also acquired a painting by Goya; another by Juan de Valdés Leal; and a magnificent painting by Zurbaran. Acquisitions in the Dutch School included paintings by Saenredam, Jan van Scorel, Jacob van Ruisdael, and Lucas van Leyden. And, of course, Mr. Kress continued to add to his brother's Italian paintings. These included *The Coronation of the Virgin* by Paolo Veneziano, one of the founders of the Venetian School; two of the most impressive portraits painted by Titian, one of *Doge Andrea Gritti* and the other of *Admiral Vincenzo Capello;* and paintings by Paolo Veronese and by Tintoretto, whose *Conversion of Saint Paul* is especially notable.

One of the most beautiful paintings to come to the Gallery is the tondo, *The Adoration of the Magi,* attributed to Fra Angelico and Filippo Lippi. Another masterpiece is Botticelli's portrait of *Giuliano de'Medici,* the younger brother of Lorenzo the Magnificent. There is the *Madonna and Child,* which has been attributed to the Circle of Verrocchio but is thought by many critics to be by the hand of Leonardo da Vinci. There is also a fine portrait by Sebastiano del Piombo and paintings of the seventeenth and eighteenth centuries such as that of *Saint Cecilia and the Angel* by Gentileschi and others by Donato Creti, Canaletto, Sebastiano and Marco Ricci, Guardi, and Bellotto.

In the field of sculpture the later Kress gifts brought to the Gallery important groups of Italian Gothic and Renaissance sculpture. Particularly notable are the two life-size polychrome wood figures by Nino Pisano, both wonderfully preserved; Verrocchio's bust of *Lorenzo de'Medici,* which makes a marvelous pair with the Verrocchio bust of *Giuliano de'Medici* in the Mellon Collection. Another

El Greco, Laocoön, *Samuel H. Kress Collection*

masterpiece is the marble bust by Bernini from the Barberini Collection in Rome; and there is a large marble *Tabernacle* by Desiderio da Settignano, a marble *Eagle* of the Hellenistic period, and a bronze bust of *Charles V* by Leone Leoni. The Kress Collection also includes important works by French sculptors, such as Carpeaux, Bouchardon, Falconet, Clodion, Pajou, and Houdon.

Still another important addition to the Kress Collection was the group of over 1,300 Renaissance bronzes which came to the Gallery in 1951. Included in this group are statuettes, plaquettes, and medals which had been brought together by the French collector, Gustave Dreyfus, and later came into the hands of the Samuel H. Kress Foundation. This famous collection was given a special installation in the Gallery that shows these beautiful small works of art to advantage.

The Kress Collection is not confined to Washington. In accordance with Samuel Kress' wish to exchange some of the works of art included in his original donation, Rush Kress and the trustees and staff of the Kress Foundation, in close cooperation with the trustees and staff of the National Gallery, arranged to give groups of beautiful and well-known paintings and sculpture to twenty art museums and to several universities and colleges throughout the United States in exchange for other works of art given to the National Gallery by the Kress Foundation. I think one is justified in saying that never before in the history of the world have such imagination and generosity been shown in bringing great art to the people of an entire country, continental in extent.

In looking back over what has been accomplished in these few years by Samuel H. Kress and his brother, Rush H. Kress, and the trustees and staff of the Kress Foundation, their achievement seems almost incredible when one takes into consideration the difficulties of acquiring great works of art under present conditions.

XII

The Widener Collection

Mr. Mellon had talked with Joseph Widener about the plans Mr. Mellon had in mind for a National Gallery, and Mr. Widener had expressed interest, particularly because his father, Peter A. B. Widener, had conceived a plan for a national gallery and had actually looked at possible sites on the Mall in Washington. But nothing had been decided; and during the spring of 1937, before Mr. Mellon died, Joseph Widener had gone directly from his house in Palm Beach to Philadelphia and Paris, without stopping in Washington to discuss Mr. Mellon's plans with him.

The Philadelphia Museum, of course, wanted the Widener Collection, with its fourteen Rembrandts, its two Vermeers, its El Grecos, Raphael, and Bellini's *The Feast of the Gods,* finished by Titian— which is one of the greatest paintings in America. In the collection are also a few nineteenth-century paintings, such as Manet's *Dead Toreador* and works by Corot, Degas, Renoir, and others. And there were English paintings by Gainsborough, Reynolds, and fine examples of the work of Turner and Constable.

I could not blame Fiske Kimball, Director of the Philadephia Museum, or his trustees for doing everything possible to secure the collection. But Joseph Widener remembered his father's and his own feeling that the country needed a great National Gallery in Washington and that it could be brought into existence only by the generosity and patriotism of men such as Mr. Mellon and himself.

I had, of course, seen the Widener Collection and realized its importance, particularly for the National Gallery, which at that time

Donatello, The David of the Casa Martelli, *Widener Collection*

Jean-Antoine Houdon, Alexandre Brongniard, *Widener Collection*

Jan Vermeer, A Woman Weighing Gold, *Widener Collection*

Giovanni Bellini, The Feast of the Gods, *Widener Collection*

97

Rembrandt van Ryn, The Mill, *Widener Collection*

had no prospects other than the Mellon Collection. During the winter of 1937, David Bruce and I had made a special trip to Lynnewood Hall, the Widener house at Elkins Park, near Philadelphia, and had the opportunity to examine the works of art at our leisure, with Miss Edith Standen, the Curator of the Collection. Mr. Mellon on one or two occasions had dined at Lynnewood Hall, and was greatly impressed with the beauty and quality of the works of art, as was everyone who saw them.

Under his father's will, Joseph Widener had been given power of

Joseph Mallord William Turner, Keelmen Heaving in Coals by Moonlight,
Widener Collection

appointment to give the Widener Collection "to any museum now
or hereafter established in the City of Philadelphia, the City of Washington, or the City of New York." It was also provided in Peter
Widener's will that his estate should not bear any part of the tax
which might be imposed on the gift of the collection either to Philadelphia or elsewhere.

It was a very reasonable condition but it posed something of a problem if the collection were given to the National Gallery. In that case,
a five-percent tax on the then value of the collection must be paid to

the State of Pennsylvania. There was no way of knowing what valuation might be placed on the collection or whether the federal government would pay such a tax; and certainly it was not to be expected that The A. W. Mellon Educational and Charitable Trust would pay a tax on another collection. There were two other difficulties. Mr. Widener wanted his collection to be shown as a unit in contiguous rooms on the main floor; and he wanted to include his Chinese porcelain and certain objects of decorative art as well as furniture.

A fundamental policy, established by Mr. Mellon and affirmed by the trustees of the National Gallery, was that no collections should be shown as a unit. I explained this situation to Mr. Widener. I also said that arrangements had already been made with Mr. Kress that his collection would not be shown as a unit, as Mr. Kress had at first wished, but that no other works of art would be shown in rooms that were entirely filled by paintings or sculpture of the same school and period donated by him. I told Mr. Widener that a room or rooms would be devoted to his superb Rembrandts but that this room, as well as his other rooms of Dutch paintings, must adjoin the rooms containing the Rembrandts and Dutch paintings in the Mellon Collection. I also pointed out that in another part of the building the same arrangement would be made for his English paintings. My Board of Trustees had approved this arrangement in the case of the Kress Collection; and when I explained all this to Mr. Widener, he, too, agreed, saying that he wanted the public to enjoy his collection in the most intelligent way.

I sympathized with Mr. Widener's desire that his collection of Chinese porcelain should go to the National Gallery with the paintings and sculpture. Mr. Widener had told me how he and his father had worked for fifty years and at great cost to bring together the beautiful late Chinese porcelains in green, white, red, and mauve; also his rare objects in crystal and enamel, and some of his finest Italian and French furniture, which he hoped could be shown as part of his collection. At Mr. Widener's invitation, Paul Mellon and I had lunched with Mr. Widener at Lynnewood Hall on December 12, 1938, when he told us how greatly he cared about his porcelains and other works of art.

When Paul Mellon and I went back to Washington, we urged the trustees to accept the porcelain, crystal, tapestries, and furniture, which they agreed to do and to place them in rooms on the ground floor. There they would not be out of scale with the paintings and sculpture to be shown on the second or main floor.

I returned to Lynnewood Hall a few days later and told Mr. Widener of these arrangements which the trustees had approved. I showed him the space on the ground floor where his porcelains would be placed, adjoining the rooms containing his small bronzes, one by Benvenuto Cellini, and the twelfth-century chalice made for Abbot Suger of St. Denis. Mr. Widener was overjoyed. He wanted to see just how they would be exhibited.

I telephoned the architect, Otto Eggers, in New York, and asked him to join me at Lynnewood Hall. Meanwhile, I had drawn on a yellow pad the shape and size of the rooms to be set aside on the ground floor of the National Gallery for Mr. Widener's collection of decorative arts. When Mr. Eggers arrived he made a sketch showing how the rooms would appear. I asked Mr. Eggers to prepare color renderings showing the rooms with travertine walls, black marble floors, and vitrines with mirrors set into the walls, each vitrine to contain a group of the Widener porcelains just as they were arranged in Lynnewood Hall. He was also to prepare renderings showing the arrangements to be made for the small bronzes; the tapestries, including the famous Cardinal Mazarin tapestry, and the furniture, all of which were to be shown in the ground floor rooms.

In three days Mr. Eggers had his color renderings ready; we returned to Lynnewood Hall; and as Mr. Widener looked at the drawings his eyes filled with tears. "If you will do this for my porcelains," he said, "You can have everything else and I will ask no questions."

Later, in January 1939, John Walker and I, with Mr. Young of Eggers & Higgins, spent several days working with Miss Standen, Curator of the Widener Collection, to arrange each of the rooms in which the Widener paintings and sculpture would be shown on the main floor and the objects of decorative art on the ground floor of the National Gallery.

Mr. Widener had taken great pains and spared no expense in providing the setting for all his works of art in Lynnewood Hall, his house at Elkins Park near Philadelphia. He had great taste and was a perfectionist in every sense of the word. He was delighted when I showed him the architectural drawings of the rooms where his paintings would be hung. He was particularly pleased with the circular travertine-covered room off the West Garden Court, which had been designed as a setting for his marble statue of *David* by Donatello, known as *The David of the Casa Martelli*.

Mr. Widener wrote a letter to the trustees of the National Gallery, agreeing to leave his collection to the Gallery. The Philadelphia Museum, still hoping to get the Widener Collection, secured legislation in June 1939, exempting educational and cultural institutions in the State of Pennsylvania from payment of tax on bequests. An effort was made by friends of Mr. Mellon and the National Gallery to have the law amended in order to grant exemption from the state tax to any public institution or museum supported by the federal government. The Philadelphia Museum, its trustees, and director fought the amendment and it was defeated in the Pennsylvania Legislature at Harrisburg.

This was the situation when the National Gallery was formally opened on the evening of March 17, 1941.

XIII

The National Gallery Is Opened to the Public

By March 1, 1941, the building for the National Gallery of Art had been completed and the Mellon and Kress Collections, a group of American paintings from the Chester Dale Collection, and other gifts had been installed. The trustees asked President Roosevelt to name a date when it would be convenient for him to open the Gallery. He selected March 17th or 31st. The earlier date was finally chosen because war clouds were gathering and we dared not wait a day longer than necessary.

Mr. Widener had sent his famous collection of acacias, dripping with yellow blossoms, which completely filled the two large sculpture halls and foreshadowed things yet to come. There was an invocation by The Reverend ZeBarney Phillips, Chaplain of the Senate. Chief Justice Charles Evans Hughes, Chairman of the Board of Trustees, presided and spoke briefly. Paul Mellon, on behalf of his father and the trustees of The A. W. Mellon Educational and Charitable Trust, presented the Gallery and the Mellon Collection to the nation. In his speech Mr. Mellon expressed the hope that the National Gallery "would become not a static but a living institution, growing in usefulness and importance to artists, scholars, and the general public." Samuel H. Kress then presented the Kress Collection and President Roosevelt accepted the Gallery and the Mellon and Kress Collections on behalf of the people of the United States. The President, in an eloquent speech, said in part:

It is with a very real sense of satisfaction that I accept for the people of the United States and on their behalf this National Gallery and the collections it contains. The giver of the building has matched the richness of his gift with the modesty of his spirit, stipulating that the Gallery shall be known not by his name but by the nation's. And those other collectors of paintings and of sculpture who have already joined, or who propose to join, their works of art to Mr. Mellon's—Mr. Kress and Mr. Widener—have felt the same desire to establish, not a memorial to themselves, but a monument to the art they love and the country to which they belong....

But though there have been many public gifts of art in the past, the gift of this Natonal Gallery, dedicated to the entire nation and containing a considerable part of the most important work brought to this country from the continent of Europe, has necessarily a new significance. It signifies a relation—a new relation here made visible in paint and in stone— between the whole people of this country, and the old inherited tradition of the arts. And we shall remember that these halls of beauty, the creation of a great American architect, combine the classicism of the past with the convenience of today....

Whatever those paintings may have been to men who looked at them a generation back— today they are not only works of art. Today they are the symbols of the human spirit, and of the world against which armies now are raised and countries overrun and men imprisoned and their work destroyed.

To accept, today, the work of German painters such as Holbein and Dürer and of Italians like Botticelli and Raphael, and of painters of the Low Countries like van Dyck and Rembrandt, and of famous Frenchmen, famous Spaniards—to accept this work today on behalf of the people of this democratic nation is to assert the belief of the people of this nation in a human spirit which now is everywhere endangered and which, in many countries where it first found form and meaning, has been rooted out and broken and destroyed.

To accept this work today is to assert the purpose of the people of America that the freedom of the human spirit and human mind which has produced the world's great art and all its science shall not be utterly destroyed....

The dedication of this Gallery to a living past, and to a greater and more richly living future, is the measure of the earnestness of our intention that the freedom of the human spirit shall go on.

The Marine Band played the National Anthem and the ceremonies were concluded in half an hour out of deference to the large audience, which was obliged to stand. Then everyone dispersed to view the collections and the building. It was a gala evening and there was an air of excitement and pleasure but also a feeling of solemnity and foreboding that pervaded the occasion.

Meanwhile there were things to do about the National Gallery. Mr. Hughes had resigned his office as Chief Justice to take effect July 1, 1941, and Supreme Court Justice Harlan F. Stone had been appointed to succeed Mr. Hughes and so became Chairman of the Gallery's Board of Trustees. David Bruce was re-elected President and Ferdinand Lammot Belin, Vice President.

XIV

The Widener Collection Comes to the

National Gallery

In particular there were things to do about the Widener Collection. Since the Pennsylvania Legislature had refused to exempt the federal government from the payment of taxes on the gift of the Widener Collection to the National Gallery, bills were introduced in Congress on August 25, 1942, with the blessing of the Roosevelt Administration, authorizing the trustees of the National Gallery to accept the Widener Collection, the United States Government to pay the tax to the State of Pennsylvania. Huntington Cairns, who was then in the Treasury Department, was very helpful in making these arrangements.

Hearings were held before the Committees on Public Buildings and Grounds of the Senate and the House of Representatives at which a number of persons testified as to the rarity and value of the Widener Collection. I testified, as did John Walker, and others, pointing out the great importance of the Widener Collection in the field of art and that it was almost essential for the National Gallery. The bill was passed authorizing the trustees of the National Gallery to accept the Widener Collection, the United States Government agreeing to pay the tax, amount not known.

President Roosevelt had announced in August 1942 that Mr. Widener had given his collection to the nation. Mr. Widener had signed a trust indenture by which part of the Widener Collection was to come to the National Gallery immediately and the remainder at his death. He, quite naturally, wanted to keep his house at Elkins Park at least partly filled with his works of art, while giving to the Gallery some of his paintings at once, as he wanted to see some of his pictures in place in Washington.

The time was fortunate. Owing to the Depression, numerous experts from New York and elsewhere placed a lower valuation on the collection than would be the case today. In any event the tax fixed and agreed to by the State of Pennsylvania was $307,630.50, which the Congress paid.

Several Philadelphians came to the Widener opening, among them Fiske Kimball, the Director of the Philadelphia Museum, and his wife. I could well understand how difficult it was for them. We had remained friends through it all and I admired Mrs. Kimball for her scholarly work in writing the *Life of Thomas Jefferson*. She had finished two volumes which she had signed and given to me. They stayed several times with us in Georgetown and we had delightful visits at Lemon Hill, their big house in Fairmount Park, near the Philadelphia Museum.

Later, in 1951, Fiske Kimball invited me to make a speech at the celebration of the 75th anniversary of the founding of the Philadelphia Museum. I was happy to feel that I had been forgiven and taken back into the fold. I had lived for two years in Philadelphia before World War I and it was my favorite city after Washington.

But all that did not affect my feeling of responsibility to get for the National Gallery the greatest paintings I could find, regardless of where they were or how difficult it might be to acquire them. I always remembered the advice given me early in my career as a museum director by the director of a museum in Europe. "Sometimes," he said, "the going will be very rough. You will wish you had never become a museum director. But don't let that bother you. Only one thing is important. When the smoke clears away, *be sure you have the pictures.*" And that I never forgot.

In the spring of 1943, on his way back to Philadelphia from Palm Beach, Mr. Widener stopped in Washington to lunch with me at the National Gallery and to see his pictures. He died that autumn, in

October 1943, and, in the months following, the remainder of the Widener Collection was brought from Lynnewood Hall and installed in the places prepared for it in the National Gallery. All was done exactly as Mr. Widener had wished. His son Peter A. B. Widener, his nephew George D. Widener, and his friend and counsel Schofield Andrews, were very helpful in making all these arrangements.

The Widener Collection, with its paintings, sculpture, drawings, enamels, Chinese porcelain, tapestries, and furniture, adds enormously to the importance of the National Gallery and gives great pleasure to all who view this remarkable collection of works of art.

XV

The Chester Dale Collection

There were a few paintings by French artists in the Mellon Collection and also a few by nineteenth-century French artists in the Widener Collection. Duncan Phillips, a trustee of the Gallery and a most discriminating collector of French paintings, as may be seen in the Phillips Memorial Gallery which he established in Washington, had given to the National Gallery a fine painting by Daumier entitled *Advice to a Young Artist*. But with these few exceptions, there were no works by French Impressionist and Post-Impressionist painters which so appeal to the public today. Mr. Mellon realized the importance of French nineteenth-century paintings; but when several were offered to him by dealers he said, "No, I hope others, who know this School better than I do, will contribute such works to the National Gallery."

One of the greatest collections of French Impressionist and Post-Impressionist paintings in this country had been brought together over many years by Chester Dale and his wife, Maud Dale, of New York. Mrs. Dale was herself an artist and had a scholarly and comprehensive knowledge of French and American painting.

Stephen Pichetto, who was Mr. Dale's restorer as well as Mr. Kress', asked Mr. and Mrs. Dale if he might bring John Walker and me to see them and their collection. They very kindly agreed to this suggestion and we were deeply impressed by the splendid collection of French works of art to be seen in the Dale's house on 79th Street in New York.

Both were interested in Mr. Mellon's plans for a National Gallery and offered to give to the new institution, at the time it was first opened to the public in 1941, some of their American paintings, which our trustees were delighted to have.

Later, as Mr. and Mrs. Dale became more familiar with the Gallery, they agreed to send to Washington on loan a large and important collection of works by French Impressionist and Post-Impressionist painters, illustrating the general development of French painting from David to Cézanne.

The Chester Dale Collection had long been recognized as one of the most distinguished collections of French nineteenth-century paintings to be found in private hands anywhere in the world. Many of the important paintings had been seen in exhibitions in this country; and the French Government had frequently asked for loans of paintings from the collection, including many of those sent to Washington.

The Chester Dale Collection also brought to the Gallery some very beautiful works by American artists, such as George Bellows and Mary Cassatt. There were several paintings by Mary Cassatt, including *The Loge* and *The Boating Party,* which were acquistions that the National Gallery badly needed. And there were a few paintings by earlier French artists such as Boucher, Drouais, Chardin, and Boilly, also paintings by El Greco and Rubens.

Manet's great painting *The Old Musician* was one of Mr. Dale's most important acquisitions. He told me how he had acquired an option on the painting and then told Mrs. Dale about it. "You do think it is a great painting, don't you?" he asked his discriminating wife. "Why, of course I do, Chester, but what has the painting to do with you?" "Well, I have bought it," said Chester Dale, "and I just wanted to be sure you liked it."

His twentieth-century paintings, including some of the finest Picassos and Matisses, he placed on loan with the Chicago Art Institute. After a year or two he decided that he would like to see his paintings under one roof and proposed to me that he bring the Chicago loans to the National Gallery. He explained to his Chicago friends why he was transferring his paintings to Washington and went ahead and did so, with the result that one can see French paint-

Édouard Manet, The Old Musician, *Chester Dale Collection*

ings of the nineteenth and twentieth centuries in Washington as in few places in the world.

Chester Dale was for several years President of the National Gallery, which became his dominant interest. After Mrs. Dale's death, he married a charming and intelligent lady, Mrs. Mary Bullard, who was of great help to him and to the Gallery in all his later donations and activities.

When he died, he left to the National Gallery all his paintings, including the ones he had sent to the Gallery on loan, as well as those

Auguste Renoir, A Girl with a Watering Can, *Chester Dale Collection*

Pablo Picasso, Family of Saltimbanques, *Chester Dale Collection*

Paul Cézanne, Still Life, *Chester Dale Collection*

he had kept in his apartment in the Plaza Hotel in New York; and he also left a generous endowment.

One of the happiest features of Chester Dale's life was the friendship which he maintained with several of the artists represented in his collection. He commissioned a number of them to paint pictures for him, as in the case of Salvador Dali's *Sacrament of the Last Supper*, and portraits of *Chester* and *Maud Dale* by the American artist, George Bellows.

Chester Dale was a strong character and life around him was never dull. He shared our love for the National Gallery and contributed greatly toward making it what it is today.

XVI

The Rosenwald Collection

The war brought many headaches to the National Gallery. But it also brought many blessings, one being Lessing J. Rosenwald, now a trustee of the Gallery and donor of the Rosenwald Collection of prints, drawings, and miniatures, one of the greatest collections in its field in the world.

Mr. Rosenwald and his wife live at Jenkintown, near Philadelphia. There they built a safe and fireproof repository for their collection of more than 22,000 engravings, drawings, etchings, lithographs, mezzotints, drypoints, miniatures, woodcuts, rare books, and reference library.

Mr. Rosenwald came to Washington to work during World War II. He was a frequent and welcome visitor to the National Gallery and soon realized the Gallery's need for a print collection such as he was in a position to provide. We at the Gallery were overjoyed when he decided to give his collection of prints and drawings to the National Gallery and his rare books and reference library to the Library of Congress. His first gift of 6,500 prints and drawings was made to the National Gallery on March 15, 1943. An exhibition was held immediately, and many exhibitions thereafter. His gifts now amount to more than 22,000 prints and drawings.

Mr. Rosenwald suggested, and the Gallery's trustees agreed, that the Rosenwald Collection should remain in the repository in Jenkintown and that the National Gallery's Curator of Prints, Miss Elizabeth Mongan, should also remain in Jenkintown where she would be available to bring selections from the Collection to Washington for

William Blake, Queen Katherine's Dream, *Rosenwald Collection*

116

Martin Schöngauer, St. Sebastian, *Rosenwald Collection*

Albrecht Dürer, The Holy Family with Three Hares, *Rosenwald Collection*

exhibition at the National Gallery, and to advise Mr. Rosenwald of the availability of rare prints that might come on the market in this country and Europe. Mr. Rosenwald would frequently exchange one of his prints for a finer impression that might come into his hands. He continued constantly to add to his collection until now it has become known throughout the world.

Mr. Rosenwald has been able to make a number of extraordinarily valuable acquisitions. In the 1920's he purchased many of the great prints from the collection of the former King of Saxony, August Friedrich. Another acquisition was the Linnell Collection of works by William Blake. These prints and drawings once belonged to Blake's pupil and friend, John Linnell. In 1937 the heirs decided to sell the Collection and Mr. Rosenwald was able to acquire it and bring these treasures to America.

Shortly afterward he bought a unique group of more than three hundred of the early woodcuts. It contains examples of such importance and rarity that the National Gallery has become one of the centers for the study of the beginning of printmaking.

The beginning of engraving, as well as woodcutting, is illustrated by rare and sometimes unique prints in the Rosenwald Collection. There is a good impression of the famous *Battle of the Naked Men* by Antonio Pollaiuolo; and several prints by one of the greatest Italian engravers, Andrea Mantegna. Two of the most celebrated German engravers of the fifteenth century, The Master E.S., and Martin Schöngauer, are represented by outstanding examples of their work. The Schöngauer Collection contains eighty-nine prints, including superb impressions of the *Flight into Egypt*, the *Angel of the Annunciation*, and the celebrated *Saint Sebastian*. The collection of Dürer's works contains nearly all his important engravings and woodcuts, and the same is true, but to a lesser extent, of the rare prints of Lucas van Leyden. There are two hundred and forty-three by Nanteuil, thirty-three portrait etchings by van Dyck, and outstanding prints by other seventeenth-century masters.

One of the most important segments of the Collection is the great group of Rembrandt's prints and drawings. The Mellon and the

Widener Collections show Rembrandt's paintings in number and quality rivalling even the national collections of The Netherlands. The Widener Collection also contains a number of Rembrandt's drawings. Now, with the addition of the Rosenwald and Gallatin Collections, Rembrandt, as draftsman and etcher, is magnificently shown at the National Gallery. There are in the Rosenwald Collection, three hundred and twenty-four etchings by Rembrandt, and eight drawings, including the famous self-portrait in sanguine.

Painters and printmakers of the nineteenth and twentieth centuries who are well represented are Picasso, Munch, Feininger, Matisse, and a number of British and American printmakers including Baskin, the American artist. Mr. Rosenwald also gave a group of bronze sculpture by Daumier.

Mr. Rosenwald organized a National Print Council, which arranges for loan exhibitions to be shown at museums throughout the country. Its main purpose is to aid the uninitiated in understanding and acquiring original prints as an important expression of fine art.

XVII

Booth and Frelinghuysen Gifts

One of the few important collections of old masters still remaining in private hands was that of Mrs. Ralph Harman Booth of Detroit. She and her husband had brought together a remarkable collection of paintings by Renaissance masters and especially by German artists, the latter being particularly rare in this country. Mr. and Mrs. Booth had bought the paintings for their own enjoyment in their house at Grosse Pointe, near Detroit.

John Walker had known their son and daughter, who arranged with their mother for us to see the collection. Mrs. Booth was interested in the National Gallery and in 1942 gave a fine example of Greek sculpture and two important Rhenish reliefs.

She had several paintings which would be great additions to the National Gallery's collection. One was a *Madonna and Child* by Giovanni Bellini, which, as Bernard Berenson once said, "had scarcely ever been surpassed by that artist." Even more desirable, in my eyes, was a *Portrait of a Youth* by Boltraffio. It was a very sensitive interpretation of a rather melancholy young man, who had apparently lost one arm. There was also a *Madonna and Child* by Tintoretto, and rare paintings by German masters, such as Cranach, Bernard Strigel, and Nicolaus Kremer.

One day when I was talking with Mrs. Booth at Grosse Pointe, she said: "If I should give you a choice of these eight paintings, which would you take?" I said, "That would put me in an awful dilemma. I think I ought to say the Bellini *Madonna and Child*, but the one I really like best is the Boltraffio." "Well," said Mrs. Booth with a smile, "I will take you out of your dilemma. You can have all these paintings and you can have them at once. But take them quickly before I change my mind."

Giovanni Bellini, Madonna and Child, *Ralph and Mary Booth Collection*

Giovanni Antonio Boltraffio, Portrait of a Youth, *Ralph and Mary Booth Collection*

Francisco de Goya, Don Bartolomé Sureda, *gift of Mr. and Mrs. P. H. B. Frelinghuysen*

Francisco de Goya, Doña Teresa Sureda, *gift of Mr. and Mrs. P. H. B. Frelinghuysen*

I was overcome but I recovered enough to ring up John Walker at the National Gallery in Washington and tell him the good news and ask him to arrange at once about a truck that would bring the paintings to Washington.

John Walker made X-ray studies of Tintoretto's *Madonna and Child*, which showed that originally there had been a circle of cherubim and stars surrounding the head of the Madonna and that these had later been painted over. After being cleaned, the original design appeared and John Walker renamed the painting *The Madonna of the Stars*, which now takes its place as an important work of Tintoretto's late period.

The two paintings by Lucas Cranach are particularly beautiful and have been tentatively identified as representing *A Prince and Princess of Saxony*, the children of Duke George of Saxony. The two Strigels and the one by Kremer are fine examples of the work of these artists.

The paintings were placed on view on February 1, 1948, and are important additions to the Gallery's resources in the fields of Italian and German art.

Another friend of the National Gallery, who made significant additions to its resources, especially in the field of Spanish painting, was Mrs. Peter H. B. Frelinghuysen of Morristown, New Jersey. She was the daughter of Mr. and Mrs. H. O. Havemeyer, who assembled the famous Havemeyer Collection now in the Metropolitan Museum in New York.

In 1941, soon after the National Gallery was opened, Mr. and Mrs. Peter Frelinghuysen gave to the Gallery two paintings by Goya; one a portrait of the Spanish artist, *Don Bartolomé Sureda*, and a very fascinating one it is in its characterization of the sitter; the other is a portrait of his wife, *Doña Teresa Sureda*, equally interesting as an example of Goya's work.

The Gallery's collection has continued to grow with gifts too numerous to mention here. All the important schools of painting in Western Europe and in the United States of America are well represented by works of their great masters; and this is true also of sculpture of the Italian and French schools.

XVIII

American Paintings

It was vital that America's National Gallery should have a distinguished representation of the works of our own artists. At the time the Gallery was opened in 1941, many of the most notable American paintings were in museums and not available at any price. But we were determined to acquire the best paintings that were still in private possession, so we all got to work and eventually, while I was Director and later during John Walker's directorship, the Gallery acquired fine examples of the work of practically all American artists eligible and desirable for the Permanent Collection.

The collection which Mr. Mellon had given to the Gallery included some well-known portraits, such as Gilbert Stuart's portrait of *Washington*, and Trumbull's *Alexander Hamilton*. Both had hung in Mr. Mellon's apartment at 1785 Massachusetts Avenue during his years in Washington. And there was the Clarke Collection of American portraits, which David Bruce brought to Mr. Mellon's attention. It included Stuart's portrait of *Mrs. Yates*, possibly the finest of all Gilbert Stuart's works; and there was also Savage's *Washington Family*, depicting the Washington family on the portico at Mount Vernon. The painting is one of great interest, especially to the people of the United States; and there was a full-length portrait by Benjamin West, another by Copley, and a few more, but no Whistler or Winslow Homer or Ryder or Mary Cassatt.

We were particularly fortunate as regards Whistler. Mr. Harris Whittemore, Jr., and the Whittemore family of Naugatuck, Connecticut, gave the Gallery two full-length paintings of great importance, *The White Girl* and *L'Andalouse* by Whistler. They are two of

Gilbert Stuart, Mrs. Richard Yates, *Andrew W. Mellon Collection*

James McNeill Whistler, The White Girl, *Harris Whittemore Collection*

Winslow Homer, Breezing Up, *gift of the W. L. and May T. Mellon Foundation*

Albert Pinkham Ryder, Siegfried and the Rhine Maidens, *Andrew W. Mellon Collection*

Thomas Eakins, The Biglin Brothers Racing, *gift of Mr. and Mrs. Cornelius Vanderbilt Whitney*

Mary Cassatt, The Boating Party, *Chester Dale Collection*

the best known works from the collection formed by Harris Whitte-more, Sr., during the last decade of the nineteenth and the early years of the twentieth century. Mr. Whittemore had the benefit of advice from Miss Mary Cassatt, who was a friend of the Whittemore family; and he had also met Whistler in Paris. Shortly afterward he bought *The White Girl*, which was then, as now, one of the most famous of all Whistler's works. It was painted in 1862 and, after being refused at the Paris Salon, was shown in 1863 at the "Salon des Refusés," where it created a sensation. *L'Andalouse* was painted thirty years later and is a portrait of Whistler's sister-in-law, Mrs. Charles Whibley.

John Walker and Huntington Cairns were about to publish their first book, *Great Paintings from the National Gallery of Art:* and we had no representation of Winslow Homer's work. There was a fine ex-ample, *Breezing Up*, at a dealer's in New York and at a high price as it seemed then. No funds were available at the moment and there were no donors in sight. William Larimer Mellon of Pittsburgh, who was a nephew but like a younger brother to Andrew W. Mellon, came to our rescue and bought the painting from the dealer in New York. It duly appeared in the book and has become one of the most popular paintings in the Gallery. Another painting by Winslow Homer, *Left and Right*, came as a gift from Mrs. Ailsa Mellon Bruce and the Avalon Foundation.

Eakins is well represented in the collection by several paintings, especially a typical and very fine work, *The Biglin Brothers Racing,* which was given by Mr. and Mrs. Cornelius Vanderbilt Whitney.

In 1946 the Gallery acquired for the Mellon Collection a well-known painting, *Siegfried and the Rhine Maidens*, by Albert Pinkham Ryder.

Shortly after the Gallery was opened, it acquired two important paintings by Copley, the large group picture, *The Red Cross Knight,* and the portrait of *Sir Robert Graham*, as gifts from Mrs. Gordon Dexter, who later gave Copley's *Death of Chatham*.

When the National Gallery was opened, it had no adequate ex-ample of Sully's work. Macgill James knew of a full-length portrait of Eliza Ridgely, *The Lady With a Harp*, which hung at Hampton,

Thomas Sully, Lady with a Harp: Eliza Ridgely, *gift of Maude Monell Vetlesen*

the Ridgely house near Baltimore. Macgill was a friend of John Ridgely of Hampton, who asked us to lunch. We both admired the Sully and Mr. Ridgely agreed to sell it. When I told a friend, Mrs. Maude Monell Vetlesen, about it, she said she would be delighted to buy it for the National Gallery and that she would like to do something further for the Gallery. So later when a New York dealer had for sale Sully's full-length portrait of *Commodore Charles Stewart*, a handsome young man in all the regalia of a full-dress Naval uniform, I told Mrs. Vetlesen about him. She said to show the painting to no one until she could see it, which she promptly did and bought it.

Another important acquisition was Gilbert Stuart's *The Skater*, a full-length portrait of William Grant of Congalton, skating on the Serpentine near London. It was one of Stuart's first commissions when he went to England. John Walker located the owner, who kindly lent it to the *Retrospective Exhibition of American Painting*, which the National Gallery of Art arranged to be shown at the Tate Gallery in London in 1946. When I was in England that summer, I talked with the owner of *The Skater*, who refused to sell it; but later her daughter, who had inherited the painting, agreed that it would look better in the National Gallery with its high ceilings, and named a price at which she would sell the painting. Mrs. Ailsa Mellon Bruce bought the painting, which now can be seen in the room near the Sullys, and is an outstanding example among the large group of paintings by Gilbert Stuart owned by the National Gallery. This group of paintings by Gilbert Stuart includes two distinguished portraits, one of President *John Adams*, and the other of *Mrs. John Adams*, given by their descendant, Mrs. Robert Homans.

There are several paintings by Sargent, including a beautiful, small painting entitled *Repose*, which shows us the kind of work Sargent did for his own pleasure. A large and important painting by George Bellows, *Both Members of This Club*, was given by Chester Dale.

I have cited a few of these individual gifts to show the widespread interest in American painting and the generosity of donors in making it possible for the National Gallery to acquire so many distinguished examples of the work of our own artists.

The National Gallery received a large group of early American paintings as the gift of Edgar William and Bernice Chrysler Garbisch of New York in 1954. Colonel and Mrs. Garbisch had brought together, with great discernment, one of the largest and most comprehensive collections of early American paintings ever assembled. The paintings are in oil, watercolor, pastel, and other media, and include portraits, landscapes, still lifes, and miniatures. They give a fascinating picture of life in this country and the persons who lived here and their possessions, from the early eighteenth to the middle of the nineteenth century.

These works of art did not derive their inspiration and technique from Europe, though some were painted by artists who had come here from other countries. In the case of these transplanted artists, however, as with the native-born, they produced paintings that reflect the romanticism and optimism of this country, together with conscientious attention to details and technique.

THE INDEX OF AMERICAN DESIGN

Another addition to the Gallery's resources in the field of American art was the gift in 1943 of the Index of American Design, which was created in the 1930's by the Works Progress Administration's Federal Art Project as part of its program of providing work for artists.

John Walker and I were familiar with the Index and had talked with Archibald MacLeish, the Librarian of Congress, with respect to keeping the Index in a government institution in Washington. On April 26, 1943, I had a telephone call from an old friend, General Philip B. Fleming, United States Army, who was then serving as Administrator of the Federal Works Progress Administration. He said that he had the responsibility for finding a permanent home for the Index of American Design and would we like to have it given to the National Gallery. I said I was sure the Gallery's trustees would be delighted, which they were; and the Index was transferred to the National Gallery of Art.

The Index consists of more than 22,000 documented drawings and watercolors, tracing the history of American design in the field of crafts and folk art from the earliest days to the end of the nineteenth century. It also includes several thousand photographs and other research material.

Among the subjects represented in the Index are textiles, wood carvings, furniture, ceramics, glassware, pewter, silver and other metalwork, decorative ironwork, household utensils, floor coverings, quilts and coverlets, costumes, lighting devices, tools and other groups of objects which, because of excellence in design or perfection of craftsmanship, have enriched American life. The Index, by recording the development of these arts and crafts in different sections of the country, forms a permanent guide and source of inspiration for artists, designers, and craftsmen.

The National Gallery exhibits these watercolors from time to time and also lends them to other museums throughout the country. In 1950 the Gallery published a handsome book, containing many reproductions of paintings in the Index, several in color. The scholarly text of the book was written by Erwin O. Christensen, Curator of the Index of American Design at the National Gallery. The book contains also an introduction by Holger Cahill, formerly National Director of the Federal Art Project.

The Index, together with the Chrysler-Garbisch Collection of early American paintings, as well as many of the best works of the greatest American artists in the Gallery's Permanent Collection, make the National Gallery, as it should be, a unique center for the study and appreciation of American art.

I should add that the acquisition of Sully's portrait of Eliza Ridgely, *The Lady With a Harp,* had unexpected results for me, and for many other persons who are interested in preserving America's heritage. When Mr. Ridgely agreed to sell the painting to a donor for the National Gallery, he also showed me Hampton, his great eighteenth-century Georgian house, so appealing in its beauty and dignity, and practically unchanged in the midst of its rolling acres, after more than a hundred and sixty years. Mr. Ridgely, however, knew that its integrity as a great country house was seriously threatened by encroaching housing developments from the neighboring city of Baltimore; and he told me of his desire that Hampton should become a national monument and saved for future generations to see. So when I went back to Washington I talked with Arthur E. Demaray, Associate Director of the National Park Service, and his assistant, Ronald Lee, and found that their admiration for Hampton fully equalled mine for *The Lady With a Harp*.

In due time Mrs. Ailsa Mellon Bruce and the Avalon Foundation gave Hampton to the National Park Service, to be held in trust for the American people. In the course of my conversations with Mr. Demaray and, later, with Director Newton B. Drury and others, I learned that the Park Service felt that, while they had the authority under the Historic Preservation Act of 1935 to acquire buildings of historic and architectural importance, they could seldom do so for lack of funds. They felt the need for a nongovernmental organization, composed of persons who would be in a position to focus attention on preservation and to supplement the work which the government was doing in this field. So, with the help of George McAneny, President of the American Scenic and Historic Preservation Society, Dr. Christopher Crittenden, of the North Carolina Department of Archives and History, Dr. Waldo Leland of the American Council of Learned Societies, and Ronald Lee, we made plans for a preservation organization and I invited a number of persons or representatives of organizations interested in preservation to meet at the National Gallery and to consider plans for bringing such an organization into existence.

Out of this, evolved the National Trust for Historic Preservation, which was chartered by Congress in 1949. I served as Chairman of the Board of Trustees from 1950 until I retired in 1962, and was succeeded by Gordon Gray. The Trust has always had an able body of trustees, under whose guidance it has acquired a number of famous houses. The National Trust is growing every year in membership and influence, and is educating people in all parts of the country to preserve what is important from an architectural, scenic, and historic point of view.

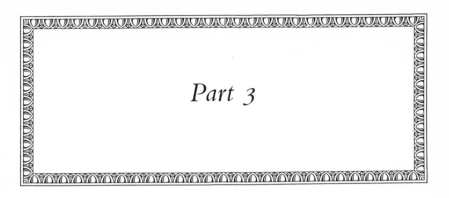

Part 3

XIX

Activities and Resources

Early in the history of the National Gallery a library was established, but with practically no books or periodicals. This was remedied by a succession of generous gifts of funds from Paul Mellon for the purchase of books for the library in the discretion of John Walker, Chief Curator, and Macgill James, Assistant Director.

The selection of books was made with special reference to the needs of the staff and with no intention of covering the entire field of the arts. The Library of Congress with its vast collections of books was nearby; and the curators and others could always go there for a book not available in the Gallery's library.

We lacked photographs and reproductions of paintings which could be used by the Gallery staff and others in Washington in research and study of the history of art. The solution to our difficulties came about in an unexpected way.

I had met Solomon R. Guggenheim of New York, the well-known industrialist, art collector, and president of the Solomon R. Guggenheim Foundation. Mr. Guggenheim had long been interested in non-objective art, and the foundation which he established maintained one of the most important museums of non-objective painting in this country. Mr. Guggenheim told me that he had a deep and patriotic interest in the National Gallery of Art and that he wanted to help in its development.

Not long after that, in the summer of 1943, the Director of the Solomon R. Guggenheim Foundation telephoned me from New York to say that Mr. Guggenheim would like to make a gift to the

National Gallery of the *Richter Archive of Illustrations on Art,* containing more than 60,000 photographs and other reproductions of paintings of all schools, with particular emphasis on Italian painting. I said I was sure that the trustees would be delighted to receive such a gift, which, of course, they were; and Mr. Guggenheim promptly gave this valuable archive to the Gallery, where it adds enormously to the library's resources for the study of attributions and art history.

The reproductions had been collected by Dr. George Martin Richter, noted authority on Giorgione and other Italian artists. The illustrations had also been arranged by Dr. Richter in accordance with the most recent and reliable discoveries in attribution and chronology of paintings.

The Richter Archive has proved of great value to students and scholars in Washington and has helped to establish a new center for the study of attributions and the history of painting.

One of the first actions taken by the Board of Trustees was the approval in February 1940 of a plan advanced by The A. W. Mellon Educational and Charitable Trust to establish a Publications Fund. Such a fund would make it possible for the Gallery to publish catalogues, books, color reproductions, and postcards of the highest quality and make them available to the public at a moderate cost. Also Christmas cards in color were published and sold in large quantities, thus fulfilling a need and also making the Gallery's paintings and sculpture known to many people over the world.

The A. W. Mellon Educational and Charitable Trust advanced the necessary funds, and the responsibility for carrying on the undertaking was placed in the hands of the Director; the Administrator, Harry McBride; the Secretary of the Board of Trustees, Donald Shepard, succeeded by Huntington Cairns; and the Chief Curator, John Walker.

The books, catalogues, color reproductions, and postcards were placed on sale in the Information Rooms on the ground and second floors. These rooms have, from the beginning, been staffed with competent men and women, who not only sell the publications but give to visitors accurate information about the works of art and their location in the Gallery.

In these rooms a general information booklet is given free of charge to visitors on request. Later, leaflets were placed in the exhibition rooms, with information about the works of art in the various rooms. There are also conducted tours of the Collection by the Curator of Education, and his able staff of docents, so that vistors may find their stay at the Gallery both intelligible and enjoyable.

Dr. Stites, who was for many years Curator of Education, conducted an unusual class, meeting once a week and comprised of wives of Cabinet officers and other officials, who wished to make a continuous study of the Gallery's collections. The class was first organized by Mrs. George M. Humphrey, whose husband was Secretary of the Treasury and a trustee ex officio of the National Gallery.

Sunday afternoon lectures are given in the auditorium, when well-known authorities discuss some phase of art, often with emphasis on the National Gallery's Collection. These lectures are financed by the Mellon Endowment Fund when given by lecturers other than members of the staff of the Gallery.

Sunday afternoon, May 23, 1947, was an unusual occasion. T. S. Eliot read selections of his poetry, including *The Wasteland, Prufrock, The Quartets,* and several others. The reading was to begin at four o'clock; by two o'clock the auditorium was filled to capacity; and an hour later there were hundreds of people waiting in the halls outside in order to see him and possibly speak to him as he passed. Many of them were young people and it made Mr. Eliot very happy to realize that they thought so highly of him and his work, and that there was such appreciation of poetry in this country.

THE A. W. MELLON LECTURES

In 1952 the Trustees of the National Gallery established an annual lecture series to be known as The A. W. Mellon Lectures on the Fine

Arts. These lectures were made possible by generous endowments from the Old Dominion Foundation, established by Paul Mellon, and the Avalon Foundation, established by Mrs. Ailsa Mellon Bruce.

The lectures are given on six successive Sunday afternoons in the auditorium of the National Gallery. They are designed to bring to the people of this country the results of the best contemporary thought and scholarship relating to the Fine Arts. The lectures are intended not only for the pleasure and information of those hearing them delivered but also for many people who will read them in books published subsequently by the Bollingen Foundation, established by Paul Mellon.

The first series of lectures was given in March and April 1952 by Jacques Maritain, internationally known philosopher. The subject of the lectures, later published in book form, was *Creative Intuition in Art and Poetry*.

Lectures were given in the following years by such eminent scholars as Sir Kenneth Clark, now Lord Clark of Saltwood. He is a former Director of the National Gallery in London, a distinguished author, and is now even more widely known as the author of his broadcasts entitled "Civilisation." Lectures were also given by Sir Herbert Read; Etienne Gilson, Director of Studies at the Pontifical Institute of Mediaeval Studies at Toronto; and Professor Ernst H. Gombrich, writer and lecturer at the Warburg Institute in London and Slade Professor of Fine Arts at Oxford; and others.

Lectures by these men and women, all distinguished in their respective fields, have increased the National Gallery's reputation as a center for the study and appreciation of art.

PUBLICATIONS

John Walker, Charles Seymour, and the other members of the curatorial staff succeeded in preparing a *Preliminary Catalogue*, which the National Gallery published in time for the opening of the Gallery in 1941. They also prepared a *Book of Illustrations*, showing paintings and sculpture in the Mellon and Kress Collections. This too was available at the opening of the Gallery in 1941.

Since that time many books have been published by the National Gallery, financed by the Publications Fund. The first of these was a very unusual one, *Masterpieces of Painting from the National Gallery of Art*. It was edited by two scholarly members of the staff, Huntington Cairns, Secretary of the Board of Trustees and General Counsel of the National Gallery, and by John Walker, Chief Curator, and later, Director. It was their idea to print opposite each color reproduction of a painting a carefully selected extract from some book of prose or poetry, which either referred to the painting or the artist or gave a short philosophical discussion of the idea embodied in the work of art. It was a novel arrangement and added enormously to the interest of the book, as well as to a better understanding of the works of art reproduced.

This first book appeared in 1944. The color reproductions showed the extraordinary number and quality of great paintings that had come to the National Gallery in the short period it had been in existence. For the first time people in this and other countries had an opportunity to know about the Gallery and its collections. I sent a copy to an English friend in London, who wrote me that it was the first book on art published during the war which she had seen and that she and her friends sat and looked at the pictures, finding it hard to believe that "such a miracle had happened in Washington."

Later there were other books such as *Masterpieces of Sculpture from the National Gallery of Art*, published in 1949, edited by Charles Seymour, Jr., and giving a review of the sculpture, especially that of the Renaissance period, in the Mellon, Kress, and Widener Collections.

In 1943 a book, *Great American Paintings*, in the National Gallery and elsewhere, was published by Oxford University Press. It was edited by John Walker and Macgill James and gives an account of paintings by American artists from 1729 to 1924.

In 1952 the Gallery published another volume, *Great Paintings from the National Gallery of Art*, edited by Huntington Cairns and John Walker. It contains, as did the first book in 1944, excellent color reproductions of paintings in the Gallery's Collection, with pertinent quotations on the opposite pages.

The Samuel H. Kress Foundation published a handsome book, *Signs and Symbols of Christian Art,* edited by George Ferguson and illustrated with many color reproductions of paintings in the Kress Collection.

An especially notable book was written by John Walker and published in 1956, *Bellini and Titian at Ferrara.* It is a scholarly and interesting study of the great painting, *The Feast of the Gods,* in the Widener Collection.

The National Gallery has continued to publish many other volumes which have greatly added to our knowledge of art and its history, usually with special reference to the works of art exhibited in the National Gallery.

XX

Care and Restoration of Paintings

One of the chief responsibilities of any well-organized art museum is the care and restoration of paintings and the use of the best available materials in doing so. Some materials used to restore damaged paintings eventually turn white, and successive applications of varnish give a dull, yellow appearance to the paintings.

The Fogg Art Museum at Cambridge, Massachusetts, especially owing to the work of Alan Burroughs, Research Fellow at the Museum, had done pioneer work in the use of X-ray to determine the condition of works of art and to study brushwork in the underpaint. But there was need for more knowledge of this subject and, in order to acquire this knowledge, the trustees of the National Gallery established an Art Fellowship at the Mellon Institute of Industrial Research in Pittsburgh, now the Carnegie-Mellon Institute. The Fellowship was made possible by grants from the Old Dominion Foundation and the Avalon Foundation with the purpose of carrying on research in varnishes and artists' materials. The National Gallery representative at the Carnegie-Mellon Institute has been a chemist, who has become familiar with the problems of restoration and especially with ingredients which would produce a clear varnish and also paints used for restoration of damaged paintings.

Francis Sullivan has been the very able Resident Restorer of works of art in the National Gallery. He uses X-ray as an aid in research and follows closely experiments in synthetic materials as developed at the Carnegie-Mellon Institute. He also gives advice on condition and care of paintings when they are brought by their owners to the National

147

Gallery. He inspects paintings on loan from the National Gallery to government buildings in Washington, and gives expert advice on special treatments to works of art belonging to other government organizations such as The White House, the Capitol, and the Treasury Department.

In 1939 Stephen Pichetto of New York was appointed Consultant Restorer of Paintings. After his death, he was succeeded by Mario Modestini, who had come from Italy and was a member of the staff of the Samuel H. Kress Foundation. Mr. Modestini has done excellent work in restoring the Kress paintings and in advising the National Gallery of Art in this difficult field. He has brought to his work not only a knowledge of paint materials but also a scholarly understanding of the history of art, which have made his work invaluable to the Kress Foundation and also to the National Gallery.

ADVICE AS TO ATTRIBUTION

As a service to the public, a qualified member of the staff gives his or her opinion as to attributions of paintings brought to the Gallery for inspection. No advice is ever given as to the market value of the paintings, that being the function of the art dealer.

INTER-AMERICAN OFFICE

During World War II, the Department of State had established an office to carry out a program for the exchange of works of art, art publications, and materials between the United States and the countries of Central and South America. In 1944 I was asked whether the National Gallery of Art would be willing to take over this program. With the approval of the trustees, an Inter-American Office was established in the Gallery, using funds supplied by the Department of State for this purpose. Porter McCray was appointed Chief of the newly established office and was succeeded later by Mrs. Margaret D. Garrett.

Various museums throughout this country participated in carrying on the program. One of the first efforts was the organization of an exhibition of forty-five American watercolor paintings for a six-month tour in countries of Latin America. The exhibition entitled *Watercolors, U.S.A.,* was mounted and assembled by the Walker Art Center in Minneapolis from a list of paintings in public and private collections proposed by the Whitney Museum of American Art in New York. Among the artists represented were Winslow Homer, John Singer Sargent, Maurice Prendergast, George Luks, Edward Hopper, John Marin, Charles Demuth, Reginald Marsh, Morris Graves, Stuart Davis, and others.

For protection of the paintings, the Walker Art Center devised an air-sealed, plexiglass frame, guaranteed to withstand the destructive effects of humidity and temperature. The exhibition was circulated by air express to cities such as Rio de Janeiro, São Paulo, Buenos Aires, Montevideo, Santiago, Lima, and Mexico City.

To accompany the exhibition, the Walker Art Center prepared an illustrated monograph containing brief biographies of the artists, whose work was included in the exhibition, as well as a survey of American watercolors within the period represented. A catalogue was provided with English, Spanish, and Portuguese text.

I give these details to show how carefully the work was done and not solely by the National Gallery but with the cooperation of other American museums. There were other exhibitions during the three years the work was carried on with diminishing funds from the Department of State. At last, the funds allocated were so small that it was not worth while to continue the work and the Inter-American Office was closed.

ART FOR AMERICAN EMBASSIES

Unfortunately there was practically no art permanently on display in our embassies abroad. The government furnished mirrors but ambassadors were expected to bring their own paintings and other works of art. There were a few ambassadors, such as Andrew W. Mellon and John Hay Whitney, who had great collections with which they decorated their embassy residences and gave to foreigners some idea of the quality of works of art that are in this country.

The Commission of Fine Arts, of which I was Chairman, in May 1953, in its Report to the President on *Government and Art,* made the following recommendation:

> *The Commission feels that it is of the utmost importance that our embassies and legations abroad should be provided with fine examples of painting and sculpture by American artists, and also furniture and other decorative arts that have been produced in this country.*

But nothing was done about it. So members of the staff at the National Gallery made some modest efforts in this direction.

As early as 1947 a prospective ambassador to Great Britain asked us to secure at least two full-length portraits, one of General Washington and the other of Thomas Jefferson, for the London embassy. We were unable to secure original portraits, so we induced a friend to have copies made of Gilbert Stuart's *Washington* in The White House and Sully's *Thomas Jefferson,* also to give a portrait, painted from life, of General Eisenhower. Other countries follow this procedure in providing copies where large original portraits of their Kings and Queens and other famous persons are not available for use in their embassies.

The National Gallery secured from other donors prints by Audubon and etchings by Whistler, also paintings by well-known American Indian artists, such as Gerald Nailer and Allen Hauser. Mrs. Chester Dale gave three paintings for the embassy in Paris; Mrs. Edward Bruce gave a landscape painting by her husband; and several donors contributed to the purchase of a painting of *Mount Vernon* by Ogden Pleissner for an overmantel in one of the rooms in the American embassy in London. There were other landscape paintings given by the widows of American artists and these are now scattered in various countries.

An organized effort is now being made by the Department of State to secure paintings and sculpture for the embassies which we maintain around the world. In addition to the efforts of the Department of State, the International Council of the Museum of Modern Art in New York has made many works of art available on a loan basis for American embassies; and the Woodward Foundation has also made important contributions of works of art on a loan basis to our embassies in many countries.

XXI

The Concerts

During the war years, when the Gallery was first opened, we had visits from thousands of men and women in uniform, in addition to all our other visitors. They came from the big camps near Washington, several of them embarkation camps, with wives or mothers or sisters who had come for a last visit with them. We made an effort to advertise the Gallery and soon the news was passed by word of mouth that the Gallery was a pleasant place to come—warm in winter and cool in summer, with a good cafeteria and, incidentally, interesting pictures. Often these men and women had leave for the day in Washington, with no hotel, so they stayed for hours in the Gallery. Few people can look at works of art intelligently and enjoy them for more than an hour or two. After that one should go somewhere, sit down and then come back later for another visit. We needed something more to offer these men in uniform.

About this time, I had a visit from Mrs. Walter Bruce Howe, an old friend of mine and also a composer of music, known in the art world as Mary Howe. She suggested free Sunday evening concerts, similar to those being given in the National Gallery in London under the direction of Dame Myra Hess. We agreed that the concerts would have a unique setting in one of our garden courts with their fishtail palms and flowers and fountains. I had some doubts about the acoustics, but they proved not too bad, though certainly not perfect. And, as compensation, we had the beauty of the garden courts instead of the lecture hall on the ground floor of the Gallery.

I explained the need to Chester Dale, who saw at once the opportunity the Gallery had to render a great service to our armed forces and to others on Sunday evenings. He offered to finance twelve concerts as an experiment. We arranged with a group from Washington's National Symphony Orchestra to play. The concerts were such a success that the trustees decided to continue them indefinitely and to finance them from the Endowment Fund provided by Mr. Mellon. In later years contributions were also made by the Calouste Gulbenkian Fund, the William Nelson Cromwell Fund, and the Music Performance Trust Fund of the Recording Industry. The Gallery secured the services of Richard Bales, who was placed in charge of the concerts. He proved to be a very talented conductor and he further has the ability to arrange concerts by orchestras, quartets, pianists, and singers that are interesting and within the Gallery's budget limitations.

Richard Bales is also a composer. He brought together the music of the Confederacy in the War Between the States, which was played with great success, first in the National Gallery, and then elsewhere. Later he composed a similar arrangement of music of the Northern Army and subsequently of the music of the War of the Revolution.

Being completely independent of box-office problems, he could arrange programs that met his own standards of quality. He instituted a Festival of American Music during four Sunday evenings in May of each year, playing only works by American composers. Many of these compositions were heard for the first time and gave impetus to the careers of our own American composers, as loan exhibitions did to our painters.

The East Garden Court, where the concerts were given during World War II, holds about six or seven hundred chairs; these were filled every Sunday evening by eight o'clock. When the concerts began, every chair was occupied and people were standing, hoping for a vacancy. At six-thirty we collected thirty Waves, Wacs, GIs, and sailors who had come to the Gallery to see the pictures. Macgill James and his wife, Bruce, were indefatigable in finding men and women in uniform and inviting them to supper in the staff dining room and the Director's dining room near the cafeteria. We had collected funds from various friends to defray the cost of food, and very good food it was. The parties were very cheerful. The men and women in the Armed Services seemed to enjoy these occasions, and went afterward to the Garden Court to hear the concerts.

I was usually at these suppers and so was my wife. One evening a young GI asked about the "million dollar picture," as he called Raphael's *Madonna of the House of Alba,* which Mr. Mellon had bought from The Hermitage for something over that amount. I explained that the painting had been sent away for safety during the war. "I am sorry," said the GI. "I certainly would like to see it. It must be a very large picture!" I said, "No, it is not very large, about thirty-six inches in diameter." "Then why did Mr. Mellon pay so much money for it?" said my GI friend. "Size has nothing to do with it," I replied, and looking toward his wife, a pretty, slim young woman, I said: "Would you like your wife better if she should weigh three hundred pounds?" He saw the point and I hope from that moment his art education began.

Except during the months of July and August, the concerts have been given every year on Sunday evenings and have contributed greatly to the enjoyment and understanding of music on the part of the people of Washington and visitors from out of town. An even larger audience has had the benefit of these concerts by means of broadcasting and tape recording.

THE BALLET

One Sunday during the war, there was a gala evening at the National Gallery. Sergei Denham, Director of the Ballet Russe de Monte Carlo, had asked me to show him the Gallery and its collections. When we came to the East Garden Court, with its fountain and flowers, I said, "This is the place where concerts are given on Sunday evenings for war workers, the armed forces, and particularly for wounded soldiers in the hospitals in this area." "What a marvelous place," said Sergei Denham, "for the Ballet Russe de Monte Carlo to give a performance for the wounded servicemen. They have done this at two places in New Jersey, and I am sure they would be delighted to contribute their dancing for the wounded men here if only we can find some way to cover the travel expenses to Washington." Mrs. Ailsa Mellon Bruce heard of the plan and generously said she would give the funds needed for travel expenses.

So it was arranged that the Ballet would come to the National Gallery on Sunday, May 2, 1943, and give a performance in the East Garden Court for service men and women, including a large number from the Army and Navy hospitals in the Washington area. The program was to include dances from the *Magic Swan*, the *Nutcracker*, and a full-length, new ballet, *Rodeo*, which involved dancing by the men of the ballet dressed as cowboys.

When the Ballet arrived in Washington Sunday afternoon, it was discovered that the trousers for the *Rodeo* were missing. At last they were located in Trenton, New Jersey, where they had been taken off the train by mistake. Time was short. A friend volunteered to fly to Trenton and rescue the trousers. When he arrived there, the trunk had been put on the Congressional Express, a train due to arrive in Washington at eight o'clock. We sent a man to the Union Station to get the trunk and rush it to the Gallery. Then came word that the train would be two hours late.

The Ballet was to start at 8:30. By this time the East Garden Court was filled with hundreds of service men and women, also the Chief Justice, Chairman of our Board of Trustees, and Mrs. Harlan Stone, the British Ambassador and Lady Halifax and their son, who had been badly wounded in the war. The members of our staff were desperate. Just then our resourceful Engineer, Sterling Eagleton, came up to me, beaming, "We have plenty of blue jeans. Why don't you use them?" It was a wonderful solution and the gentlemen of the Ballet thoroughly enjoyed this novel peformance, as did everyone in the audience.

Meanwhile there was another performance going on in the Gallery at the same time. The United States Navy Band was playing in the auditorium for war workers and other civilians who were accustomed to come to the National Gallery for concerts on Sunday evenings. All ended well, but we never undertook such a hectic program again.

The Gallery gave service men and women, war workers, and everyone in Washington the pleasure of looking at great works of art and listening to fine music, as well as places to rest and read and eat in comfortable surroundings. But never lowered its "standard of excellence" as an art museum. On the contrary it made many men and women, especially in the armed services, aware for the first time of what art museums had to offer in the way of intellectual enjoyment and education in the arts.

XXII

The War Years

The war presented major problems to all museums. Our first responsibility was to preserve the works of art for which we and our trustees
were responsible. Also it was necessary (and this was particularly true
for the newly opened National Gallery) to keep on view enough objects to make the museum an interesting place for visitors.

The National Gallery had been opened on March 17, 1941, when
it seemed that war might come at any time. I was worried even then
as to what Hitler and the Japanese might do. So I went to Senator and
Mrs. Peter Gerry, who had been friends of mine for many years. I
asked, if America should become involved in the war, would they be
willing for me to take our most important paintings and sculpture to
Biltmore House, in the Blue Ridge Mountains near Asheville, North
Carolina. I had been there occasionally when Mrs. Gerry was Mrs.
George Vanderbilt, and she and her daughter lived at Biltmore
House.

The Gerrys could not have been kinder or more understanding.
They said there was a large vacant room in Biltmore House, where
we could store everything as their guests. John Walker, Harry Mc-
Bride, and I went to Biltmore to get everything in readiness. So when
the attack was made on Pearl Harbor, we were prepared; and on
New Year's Day 1942, we moved out all of our most important
works of art.

We had engaged an express car which was attached to the Sou-
thern Railway train to Asheville; and into that car we put the steel
vans which were taken out next morning at Biltmore Station and

loaded on trucks to carry them to Biltmore House. It was a long climb through the park, along winding roads, and up hills covered with ice. The trucks swayed from side to side and in my imagination I could see Raphael's *Alba Madonna* and all the rest crashing on the road. But we arrived safely; and at Biltmore everything remained in perfect condition until the war ended. A member of the staff, John Walker or Macgill James or Charles Seymour, was always there, in addition to the guards; and the Biltmore trustees could not have been kinder.

Finally the war ended and we could bring everything back to Washington. This time we brought them back in motor trucks with our own guards and also with police from North Carolina and Virginia. At the Potomac River bridge we were met by motorcycle police of the District of Columbia, who preceded our caravan down Constitution Avenue, blowing whistles and clearing away traffic. People looked at the parade in amazement and never before or since have I felt that *art* was given such importance, even over traffic. Everything was installed as before and we were able to return to their owners pictures which had been loaned to us to fill vacant spaces during the war.

COLOR REPRODUCTIONS IN CAMPS AND HOSPITALS

During the war years, owing to contributions from the Gallery's trustees and a few private donors, the National Gallery sent to libraries, hospitals, and dayrooms in the camps, in cooperation with the Camp and Hospital Service of the District of Columbia Chapter of the American Red Cross, framed color reproductions of paintings in the National Gallery. Many letters of appreciation were received from service men and women. One wrote: "In days like these, it is consoling to know that beauty and the inspiration derived from beauty are not things forgotten. These are still with us and for this we can be thankful."

Such sentiments occur frequently in messages written in a large book which we kept in the Founders Room for visitors from the Armed Services to sign. It was very inspiring to read what these men and women said about their country and all that it had given them and that they were prepared to defend it with their lives.

During the war we had frequent visits from Field Marshalls, Generals, Admirals, and other high-ranking officers of the Armed Services of our allies, who came to the National Gallery to enjoy, as they said, for a brief hour "an atmosphere free of wartime worries." Afterwards one or two of them wrote me from far-off places, voicing their longing for the National Gallery.

In addition to the color reproductions sent to the hospitals of the Armed Services, a number were sent to private hospitals for the benefit of both patients and doctors. Donald Shepard and I had visited a hospital in a small mining town in West Virginia operated by a very remarkable man, Dr. William S. Laird. He wrote me, "We have conclusive evidence of the therapeutic value of pictures in our hospital experience. . . . Members of the medical staff, nurses, and patients all bear witness to the good effects of the pictures. They are happier, more easily cared for, and more amenable to hospital routine. This has been noticed by doctors hitherto skeptical and by nurses without previous experience in wards in which pictures were displayed. So marked is this improvement that both doctors and nurses prefer duty in this ward."

With comment from such an eminent and experienced person, the National Gallery continued to send to private, as well as military, hospitals color reproductions which were contributed by individuals and by two foundations.

SALVAGING ART IN WAR AREAS

An important activity arising out of the war was the establishment of the American Commission for the Protection and Salvage of Artistic and Historic Monuments in War Areas.

It had become evident in 1942 that the Allied Armies would soon be landing on the continent of Europe to rescue the Western nations from occupation by Hitler's forces. Several groups and organizations in this country were concerned for the fate of works of art, monuments, buildings, libraries, and records which would be endangered and probably destroyed unless some form of protection could be devised.

In the autumn of 1942, the President of the Archaeological Institute of America, the President of the College Art Association, the Director of the National Gallery of Art in Washington, and the Director of the Metropolitan Museum in New York proposed to Chief Justice Harlan F. Stone, who had succeeded Chief Justice Hughes as Chairman of the Board of Trustees of the National Gallery, that a governmental commission be established for the protection of works of art and historic monuments in Europe.

On December 8, 1942, Chief Justice Stone wrote a letter to President Roosevelt asking his approval of a plan for the "creation of an organization functioning under the auspices of the Government, for the protection and conservation of works of art, and of artistic and historic monuments and records in Europe, and to aid in salvaging and returning to, or compensating in kind, the lawful owners of such objects which have been appropriated by the Axis powers or by individuals acting with their authority or consent." With his letter he enclosed a memorandum, recommending the membership of such a Commission and also suggesting that the British and Soviet Governments be asked to take parallel action in carrying out this work.

President Roosevelt approved this plan; and on April 24, 1943, wrote to Chief Justice Stone saying that the original memorandum had been shown to the Chiefs of Staff, who had agreed to assist in any way that did not interfere with their military operations.

The Secretary of State, Cordell Hull, wrote to the President, approving the establishment of such a commission and recommending that it work with the School of Military Government at Charlottesville, Virginia, in finding qualified persons who could be trained and attached to the staffs of our armies to advise concerning the care and protection to be given to artistic and historic objects in war areas. He also suggested that the offices of the Commission be in the National Gallery of Art and that the members serve without remuneration. The Secretary of War, Henry L. Stimson, also was in favor of the establishment of the Commission.

The President approved these recommendations and on August 20, 1943, the Department of State announced the establishment of "The American Commission for the Protection and Salvage of Artistic and Historic Monuments in Europe," under the chairmanship of Owen J. Roberts, Justice of the United States Supreme Court, the headquarters of the Commission to be in the National Gallery. The Commission, needless to say, was usually referred to by a shorter title, and was know as "The Roberts Commission."

As Director of the National Gallery and a member of the Commission of Fine Arts, I was appointed Vice Chairman; and Huntington Cairns, Secretary-Treasurer of the National Gallery, was appointed Secretary-Treasurer of the Commission. The other original members appointed were: Herbert H. Lehman, Director of the United Nations Relief and Rehabilitation Administration; Archibald MacLeish, former Librarian of Congress; William Bell Dinsmoor, President of the Archaeological Institute of America; Francis Henry Taylor, Director of the Metropolitan Museum of Art in New York and President of the Association of Art Museum Directors; Paul J. Sachs, Associate Director of the Fogg Museum of Fine Arts of Harvard University; and Alfred E. Smith, former Governor of New York. Mr. Smith was succeeded after his death by Francis Cardinal Spellman of New York. Mr. MacLeish resigned from the Commission upon his appointment as Assistant Secretary of State in January 1945.

John Walker, Chief Curator of the National Gallery of Art, was named Special Adviser to the Commission at the time of its creation, as was Sumner McK. Crosby of Yale University. In April 1945, Horace H. F. Jayne of the Metropolitan Museum in New York was appointed Special Adviser on matters concerning the Far East. Dr. Rensselaer W. Lee of Smith College and the Institute for Advanced Study, Princeton, New Jersey, was appointed Consultant to the

Commission in May 1945 and worked closely with it in Washington until July of that year.

In the office of the Commission established in the National Gallery in Washington, John A. Gilmore served as Administrative Officer and Assistant Secretary-Treasurer from September 1943 until his resignation in June 1945. Charles H. Sawyer, Director of the Worcester Art Museum, succeeded him in July 1945 and served until his resignation in December 1945. Charles Seymour, Jr., Curator of Sculpture at the National Gallery, assumed the responsibilities of the Assistant Secretary-Treasurer until the arrival, in February 1946, of Lamont Moore, Associate Curator of the National Gallery. William L. M. Burke, Acting Director of the Index of Christian Art at Princeton University, was director of the research project of the Commission, originally instituted by the American Council of Learned Societies.

As a result of requests from the Navy Department that the Commission prepare maps and lists of areas in the Far East containing cultural and historic monuments, the Commission was officially authorized on April 21, 1944, to change its name by the substitution of the words "War Areas" for the word "Europe."

The Commission worked closely with the American Defense-Harvard Group and the Committee for the Protection of Cultural Treasures in War Areas of the American Council of Learned Societies (both independent, civilian groups established before the creation of the Roberts Commission).

The Commission recommended to the War and Navy Departments men in the Armed Services or in private life who were qualified to advise our armed forces as to the location of historic monuments or collections of works of art which should be protected from destruction or from depredation by civilians or armed forces. Maps were supplied and at intervals reports were made by members of the Commission and others who had visited war areas and were in a position to recommend procedures to the Commission. These included Francis Henry Taylor, John Walker, Sumner McK. Crosby; also John Nicholas Brown, who had been appointed by the War

Department, on the Commission's recommendation, to go to the European theater as Adviser on Cultural Matters to the United States Group, Control Council for Germany, and was in a position to advise the Commission as to operations in this theater. Others who made valuable reports to the Commission were Major Theodore Sizer, Commander George L. Stout, Sir John Forsdyke, Director of the British Museum and a member of the (British) McMillan Committee. Horace H. F. Jayne, who served as Special Representative of the Commission in the Far East, went to China to consult with and advise the Chinese Government and the Allied military authorities in the Far East regarding the preservation and restitution of art and historic treasures in that area.

During the war the Commission was instrumental in the establishment by the War Department of a Monuments, Fine Arts and Archives program for the protection of art and historic monuments in war areas under the direction of the Civil Affairs Division of the War Department.

The Commission advised the Department of State in the formulation of principles for the restitution of artistic and historic material in the post-war period. It was also helpful in bringing about the restitution to the owner governments of looted public works of art found in the American Zone in Germany.

Not a single work of art was expropriated by the American Government, not even those acquired by Hitler and Goering under conditions far from admirable. Nevertheless, the American Government, in carrying out this policy of restitution, was subjected to unwarranted criticism by some of its own military and civilian personnel.

One day, shortly after the fighting stopped in Germany, I received a visit from a high official in the War Department, who asked whether the National Gallery would be willing to accept temporarily the custody and responsibility for the care of the collection of paintings from the Kaiser-Friedrich Museum in Berlin, which had been found by the invading American army in a salt mine in Germany. Chief Justice and Mrs. Stone were at that time in Whitefield, New

Hampshire, where they were established for the summer. I telephoned the Chief Justice, asking if I could see him the next morning about an important and confidential matter that concerned the Gallery. He said, of course, to come at once. When I arrived the next morning, the Chief Justice was out for his morning walk and met me at a little distance from the house as I drove up in a car.

As we walked along the road, I told him of the situation and the responsibility that would be imposed on the trustees of the National Gallery. The Chief Justice looked at me and said, "If the Government asks us to take care of these paintings, we must do it. It is a duty which we could not escape if we wanted to, and certainly we do not want to." I left immediately, not stopping long enough for lunch, and came back to Washington, where I told the War Department officials that the trustees of the National Gallery would accept responsibility for the German-owned paintings and would give them the same care we gave our own collection. Shortly afterward the paintings were brought to this country in an army transport and delivered to the Gallery, where they were placed in one of our air-conditioned storage rooms.

There was an outcry on the part of certain museum people and also arts and monuments officers who seemed to think the United States Government had placed itself in the position where this beneficent action on its part could be construed as looting of the German-owned art. This extraordinary point of view was set forth in the manifesto signed by a few of these individuals, notwithstanding statements which had been issued by President Truman and Chief Justice Stone at the time the paintings arrived, saying that the works of art were being stored for safety in the National Gallery and would be returned to Germany when conditions justified. Chief Justice Stone was outraged at statements challenging, as he considered it, the good faith of the American Government and also the integrity of the President and the Chief Justice of the United States. He said to me with anger in his voice, "Have these men taken leave of their senses?" The Commission also was equally outraged at the action of these people and issued a statement deploring such behavior.

Later, when conditions justified the return of the paintings to Germany, the question arose as to whether the collection should be exhibited in Washington and elsewhere in the United States. After all, the collection had been saved owing to action by the United States Army; and the Department of the Army decided that the paintings should be shown first in the National Gallery in Washington and later at other museums in this country.

The Army requested the National Gallery to select approximately fifty paintings from the collection, which were considered most likely to suffer damage or deterioration if sent on tour. A committee consisting of John Walker, Chief Curator of the National Gallery, as chairman, and directors and curators of several other museums, also a former curator of the Kaiser-Friedrich Museum, eliminated fifty-two paintings which were sent back to Germany for restoration.

The other paintings were shown in the National Gallery from March 17 to April 25, 1948. There were famous Italian paintings by Giotto, Fra Angelico, Fra Filippo Lippi, Botticelli, Raphael, Giorgione, Titian, Caravaggio, and Tiepolo. There were also notable works by Flemish, German, Dutch, and French artists, including paintings by Jan van Eyck, Rogier van der Weyden, Petrus Christus, Altdorfer, Dürer, Cranach, and Holbein, as well as fifteen Rembrandts, two Vermeers, six Frans Hals, and the work of French artists such as Fouquet, Poussin, Claude Lorrain, Chardin, and Watteau.

It was a splendid exhibition and was seen by 964,970 visitors. The rooms were so crowded that all the Very Important People asked to come from nine to ten or from five to eight o'clock when the public was not admitted. It was an exhausting experience for our staff and we were glad to see the paintings leave for other cities, though rather nervous about their safety.

According to the wishes of the Senate Armed Services Committee and the Department of the Army, the National Gallery had been given the responsibility of making arrangements for the tour of the paintings to other museums. We sent out telegrams to the directors of the larger art museums in this country, asking them to come to Washington and help to arrange the schedule. A meeting of the directors was held in the National Gallery on April 29, 1948, when these arrangements were completed and later approved by the Department of the Army. It was arranged that the paintings should go to museums in New York, Philadelphia, Boston, Chicago, Detroit, Cleveland, Minneapolis, San Francisco, Los Angeles, St. Louis, Pittsburgh, and Toledo. Then they were sent back to Germany in excellent condition, and so ended a unique chapter in art history.

As John Walker said at the time: "Never before in history have such efforts been made to care for works of art belonging to an enemy country."

XXIII

Exhibitions

Many temporary or loan exhibitions have been held in the National Gallery. I can mention only a few here, such as the Anniversary Exhibitions and collections placed on indefinite loan; also exhibitions arising out of special events, such as President Truman's Inaugural Reception.

PRE-COLUMBIAN ART

In 1947 Robert Woods Bliss placed on loan at the National Gallery his distinguished collection of Pre-Columbian art, showing the range of New World art from Mexico to Peru. The Collection included sculpture, goldsmith's work, textiles, and ceramics created by the inhabitants of the Western Hemisphere before Columbus arrived in the New World.

The Collection remained at the National Gallery for many years, eventually going to Dumbarton Oaks, to be installed in a beautiful building in the great garden as part of the donation of house, garden, and contents which Mr. and Mrs. Bliss made to Harvard University.

GULBENKIAN COLLECTION

One of the most discriminating collectors of great works of art was C. S. Gulbenkian, living after World War II in Paris and Lisbon. John Walker had met him and I later had talked with him in both

Lisbon and Paris. Mr. Gulbenkian said he would like to lend some of his works of art to the National Gallery in Washington as a gesture of appreciation for all that America had done in saving Europe from the Nazis in World War II.

In 1949 he sent his collection of Egyptian sculpture containing many pieces of great importance and beauty. Shortly afterward he sent to Washington on loan a superb group of paintings including works of the highest quality by Ghirlandaio, Carpaccio, Rubens, Rembrandt, and a beautiful painting by Fragonard, *A Fête at Rambouillet*. There were in addition examples of the work of French nineteenth-century artists such as Manet, Corot, and Renoir.

After Mr. Gulbenkian's death the collection was returned to the Calouste Gulbenkian Foundation at Lisbon, where it is now on exhibition.

PRESIDENT TRUMAN'S INAUGURAL RECEPTION

In 1949, The White House was undergoing extensive repairs. The National Gallery had accepted custody of paintings, sculpture, and furniture belonging to The White House. These were placed in the Gallery's storage rooms until they could be returned to The White House after repairs had been completed. At the request of President Truman, his Inaugural Reception was held in the National Gallery of Art on January 20, 1949. A temporary platform was built in the West Sculpture Hall where the President addressed the guests, most of whom had been received personally in the West Garden Court. The rotunda and garden courts were filled with flowers; the Marine Band Orchestra in their red coats played; and more than eight thousand people came to the Gallery on this important occasion.

MAKERS OF HISTORY IN WASHINGTON

While the White House portraits were in the National Gallery, they were shown in 1950, by courtesy of President and Mrs. Truman, as part of an exhibition *Makers of History in Washington, 1800-1950*. The exhibition was assembled with funds provided by the National Capital Sesquicentennial Commission.

In addition to the portraits of Presidents and their wives, usually seen only in The White House, the exhibition included portraits of those concerned with the development of the City of Washington, itself. For this reason a portrait of *Alexander Hamilton* was included because of the part which he played in selecting the site for the federal government. His portrait was shown in the room with those of *Washington, Jefferson,* and *Jay,* his co-workers in the far greater task of founding the Republic and organizing the Government during its early years. In another room was shown the famous group portrait by Savage, *The Washington Family,* with General and Mrs. Washington seated on the terrace at Mount Vernon, viewing the map of the proposed "Federal City" designed by Major Pierre Charles L'Enfant. This painting is part of the Mellon Collection in the National Gallery.

The portraits were arranged in chronological order, the persons represented usually being shown with others in the administrations with which they were identified. In this way the portrait of *General Robert E. Lee* was shown in the room with portraits of *President Lincoln* and *General Grant*; and that of *Henry Adams* was with the portraits of *President Theodore Roosevelt* and his Secretary of State, *John Hay,* and others in that brilliant group of friends who lived around Lafayette Square and whose writings and conversation marked such a high point in the life of Washington.

In the Introduction to the catalogue, I said:

The exhibition gives, in microcosm, a preview of what a National Portrait Gallery should be if present plans are carried out. The Trustees of the National Gallery of Art now hold a collection of portraits of historical personages as the nucleus of what, it is hoped, will some day become a National Portrait Gallery. Such a gallery is particularly needed at the present time when it is so important for the coming generation to have an understanding of our history and of those who created the civilization we now enjoy. In realizing these aims, a National Portrait Gallery would be an educational force of the greatest value, with a potential influence on future generations that could not possibly be measured.

Special exhibitions were held on the fifth, tenth, and fifteenth anniversaries of the opening of the National Gallery of Art. These exhibitions gave an opportunity to emphasize the many rare and beautiful paintings and sculpture that came to the National Gallery, owing to the efforts and the generosity of Samuel H. Kress, Rush Kress, and the Samuel H. Kress Foundation.

At the exhibition in 1946, over a hundred paintings were placed on view, includng the work of artists such as Fra Angelico, Botticelli, Veneziano, Sassetta, Cossa, and Tura. Also shown at the time was the painting entitled *Christ at the Sea of Galilee* by Tintoretto, as was Titian's portrait of *Cardinal Pietro Bembo*.

The exhibition included a group of paintings by French artists, such as Boucher, Chardin, Drouais, Louis Le Nain, and Pater. There were three paintings by Fragonard; also Claude Lorrain's *The Herdsman* and Poussin's *The Baptism of Christ*. Important works of sculpture by Desiderio da Settignano, Ghiberti, Verrocchio, and others were shown in this exhibition.

At the tenth anniversary in 1951, the additions to the Kress Collection included such celebrated paintings as *The Adoration of the Magi* by Fra Angelico and Fra Filippo Lippi; *The Dance of Salome* by Benozzo Gozzoli; superb portraits by Mantegna and Titian; and in the Flemish and French Schools two important portraits by Petrus Christus; works by Poussin and Claude Lorrain; and two paintings by Ingres, to be added to the artist's portrait of *Mme. Moitessier,* already in the Samuel H. Kress Collection. There were also paintings by Northern European masters of the fifteenth and sixteenth centuries, such as the *Madonna and Child* and a fine portrait, both by Dürer. At this time there came to the Gallery also the celebrated collection of medals, plaquettes, and small bronzes, brought together by Gustave Dreyfus and afterward acquired by the Samuel H. Kress Foundation.

The fifteenth anniversary of the founding of the National Gallery was marked by a large evening reception at the Gallery on March 17, 1956, when an important group of paintings and sculpture, acquired in the preceding years by the late Samuel H. Kress, by Rush H. Kress, and the Samuel H. Kress Foundation, were placed on view.

It was an extraordinary group of masterpiecees and greatly enhanced the prestige of the National Gallery. These works of art were viewed on the evening of March 17, by nearly twelve thousand persons.

It was my last appearance at a large function as Director of the National Gallery. I was retiring at the end of June and it gave me great satisfaction to know that the National Gallery had obtained these outstanding masterpieces, which added so much to its status as one of the world's great art museums.

XXIV

Changing of the Guard

When I reached the age of retirement, on July 1, 1955, the Board of Trustees asked me to serve an additional year, which I was glad to do, in order to complete the arrangements for the Gallery's Fifteenth Anniversary then under way.

On July 1, 1956, my friends on the staff of the Gallery gave me a farewell party in the large cafeteria. It included everyone—officers, curators, docents, technicians, and guards. I was given an eighteenth-century silver inkstand and a book autographed by everyone, both of which I deeply value as evidence of their friendship.

I was very happy that John Walker was to succeed me as Director. I told him and the others assembled on that farewell occasion that, in leaving them, I was severing all ties except those of friendship; that I would never make my successor's life a burden by incessant suggestions; and that, if he wanted advice, he could come to me. But John Walker had been with the Gallery from the beginning and no one understands better its operation and the philosophy on which the Gallery is based.

John Walker became Director of the National Gallery on July 1, 1956. He had made himself a distinguished position in the art world of this country and Europe. He had been Chief Curator of the National Gallery since 1939. He was eminently qualified by experience and personality to carry on the Gallery's development along the guidelines laid down by Mr. Mellon, the trustees, and the Act of Congress establishing the Gallery. He and I worked together in planning the installation of works of art in the building, and in the growth of the collection, on which he has left an indelible imprint of his knowledge and taste. Under him as Director, the National Gallery has continued to grow in prestige and resources and has become more important with each passing year.

As I write these words, changes have come to the National Gallery, as they do to all institutions. John Walker has retired as Director and has been succeeded by John Carter Brown, who has served as Assistant Director and has shown that he has the ability, the knowledge, and the personality to carry the National Gallery to even greater heights, as I am sure he will do.

When I left the National Gallery in 1956, I moved my own desk and other furniture, bought years ago in London, to the United States Commission of Fine Arts. I had been a member of the Commission since President Roosevelt had appointed me in 1943 and had been elected by the members as Chairman since 1950. I had been reappointed by President Truman and twice by President Eisenhower. I had carried on the work while Director of the National Gallery, but now there was leisure to give it my full attention and I enoyed doing so. None of the members receive pay and all are glad to serve their country in this way. I was to remain at the Commission until 1963, when I asked President Kennedy not to consider me for another term, as I felt that I had served long enough.

THE DIRECTOR AND THE MUSEUM

The role of an art museum director is a peculiar one. It requires knowledge of how a museum should be run and firmness in doing it, also sympathetic and careful compliance in carrying out the policies established by the trustees. I was meticulous in carrying out the policies which my trustees had established—policies with which I was familiar and sympathetic since the time when Mr. Mellon had founded the museum. The Director should keep in close contact with the members of the museum's staff, particularly the curators, and see that public recognition is given to important accomplishments made by them. He should also operate within the budget established by the trustees.

After I retired as Director of the National Gallery, I became a trustee of the Corcoran Gallery of Art and a member of the Board of two other museums. Now that I can view the situation from the angle of both trustee and director, I have come to two conclusions: first, that the trustees are responsible for defining and enforcing the policy of the museum and for raising the funds to carry it out; also for keeping the museum adequately equipped. Their second duty is to choose a director who has the ability to operate the museum to the satisfaction of the trustees, with a staff chosen by the director. In aesthetic matters, the director and his or her curators should make the decisions; and if they are not competent to do so, they should be replaced by others who are competent. But the trustees should never attempt to do the work of the director, however tempting it may be. If the museum is buying a work of art with museum funds, or accepting the gift of a work of art, then it should be with the approval of the trustees after careful consideration of the advice of the director and the curators.

I wanted the National Gallery to give training to qualified candidates for scholarly careers in art museums. And in 1959, after I had retired as director, the Old Dominion Foundation, established by Paul Mellon, and the Avalon Foundation, established by Mrs. Ailsa Mellon Bruce, provided funds for two scholarships to give training, both in Washington and abroad, to promising young men and women who wish to enter the museum profession. They were kind enough to call them the "David E. Finley Fellowships." I deeply appreciated the honor and it gives me great satifaction to know that the National Gallery is in a position to give such training to those qualified to receive it.

XXV

The Role of the Art Museum

I had my own philosophy about art museums, their purpose, and how they should function to the greatest advantage of the people for whom they were created. I had derived this in large part from Mr. Mellon, who had very definite ideas about art museums, their functioning, and especially in the maintenance of a high standard of quality in the works of art shown to the public. John Walker, Charles Seymour, Jr., and other members of the staff had the same philosophy, so there was always a happy atmosphere in the museum, with none of the intramural bickerings that sometimes mar life in such institutions.

We agreed that museums have, first of all, a curatorial function. They must preserve and protect their works of art from heat and moisture and a too inquisitive and sometimes uninformed public. At the same time art must be made accessible, so that it may be viewed as comfortably as possible and carry its message to the viewer and give pleasure.

In my own mind pleasure and education that would increase enjoyment of works of art are the two most important ends to be achieved. If the paintings and sculpture are to carry their message to the viewer, they should, if possible, be shown in rooms in scale with the works of art; and they should not be crowded, so that they and their too insistent neighbors do not impinge upon each other with chaotic results for the visitor. In my own opinion, paintings in museums should not be hung too high and should, if possible, be at eye level of the viewer; also the background should be harmonious and never distract attention from the painting.

Sculpture should be shown separately if it is of sufficient importance to deserve one's full attention. And in the National Gallery, the sculpture of great rarity and beauty has been installed to advantage in its own rooms.

We did everything we could to make the National Gallery comfortable. Most large public museums are not comfortable. They involve a great deal of walking and standing and, after an hour or two, the eye gets tired and one should go to lunch or sit down and rest. In the National Gallery there is an excellent cafeteria and there are two garden courts with their fountains and flowers. There are also two rooms where smoking is allowed, and practically all the exhibition rooms have comfortable sofas, with leaflets telling about the works of art.

Also there are wheel chairs, made of chromium and easy to manipulate. They were a novelty when the Gallery opened in 1941; at least I had never seen them until one evening, as I arrived at a dinner, a young woman, temporarily lame, was taken out of her car, with her folding wheel chair in which she was rolled in to dinner. We got a dozen of the chairs for the National Gallery "for those desiring to use them" as stated in the Gallery folder, and many did use them. That gave me the idea of chromium baby carriages to relieve long-suffering fathers whom I saw struggling through the Gallery, a baby on their shoulder. These, too, were a great success.

The day is past when museums were considered the domain of the "elite," or those with some training in the arts or in their history. One morning during World War II a young GI in uniform arrived at the door of the National Gallery just as I was going in. I asked whether he had been to the Gallery before. He said, no, he lived in Vermont and had come to Washington to report for duty with the Army but had purposely come a day earlier in order to visit the National Gallery. "I really shouldn't be here," he said. "I don't know anything about art." "Don't let that worry you," I said. "Come in and look at the pictures and find out whether any of them give you pleasure or have any meaning for you. If they do, come back and look at them again." I happened to see him later in the day in one of the rooms containing Italian paintings. "Did you find any paintings you like?" I asked him, "Oh, yes," he said, "a great many, and I would like to know more about them." He had found, I felt, the secret of art museums and the real reason for their existence.

Art museums, as well as science and history museums, have an educational role that is of the greatest importance. Research is one of their primary functions; and they also have a responsibility to make this knowledge available to the outside world through publications and also through guided tours for adults and children. In one respect the museum has a great advantage over the schools. It teaches mostly by means of objects, rather than the printed book. And this is a most appealing way of acquiring knowledge, in addition to the fact that education, as offered by the museums, is on a voluntary or take-it or leave-it basis.

The art museum has another function. It is one of the few stabilizing forces in a changing world. In museums, such as the National Gallery and others, we have a sense of continuity with the past. The really great works of art never lose their vitality and, when seen in relation to those of other ages and other peoples, they help us to form some concept of the world in which we live and the civilization we have inherited. When we are able to enjoy a work of art, created by someone belonging to another nation or race or age, we are less likely to be frightened by differences in speech and outlook and behavior among the various peoples of our own day with whom we must deal in carrying on the work of the world.

In a museum we are not impressed by ideologies so much as by human genius, with the result that we acquire that respect for personality and for the dignity of the individual which is at the very foundation of our Western civilization. These things the arts make plain to us and nowhere so clearly as in museums.

The public, in speaking of a work of art, is accustomed to think of it as being, or not being, of "museum quality." These words, I am sorry to say, are used generally with a lack of precision which indicates that there is neither a common agreement as to the meaning of the words nor a common acceptance of the values to which the words refer, since there is no rigid standard to which museums adhere in determining what is or is not museum quality.

The public is right, however, in fastening on museums the responsibility for the highest standards of integrity and mental honesty in admitting to museums only those things which are worthy to be there. The American public is fully capable of enjoying the best and it is the duty of museums to give them only the best, so far as lies within their power. In the art world, as in other fields of human endeavor, we need the discipline of high standards, rigidly adhered to.

It is, I think, a hopeful sign that the country at large is beginning to recognize that museums can be helpful in the struggle for the only kind of world that is fit to live in. For one thing, people generally are becoming aware of the fact that museums have something to offer of which many people are in dire need. In spite of all the progress that we have made from the mechanical and technological points of view, in spite of the creature comforts of our gadget-civilization, man is conscious of the fact that merely material things do not satisfy and that something more is needed if he is to avoid the feeling of frustration and incompleteness which can mar even the most successful career, as judged by worldly standards.

The man whose daily job gives him no real satisfaction and is only a means of subsisting, suffers an even greater sense of frustration and boredom. With increased leisure, due to the shorter working day, he is left with time on his hands and also time to think. When that stage is reached and he realizes that in the midst of plenty he is intellectually starved, he is quite likely to turn to the museum for stimulus as well as pleasure, if not for himself, at least for his children.

During my years at the National Gallery and afterwards, the Gallery has been visited by millions of persons from all parts of this country and the world. This increasing use of the National Gallery and of other museums throughout the country is some indication, at least, that the American people not only consider their museums important but enjoy them. This should be of some comfort to those who are too depressed about the materialistic aspects of our increasingly mechanized civilization.

I was always grateful for gifts to the National Gallery, but I never felt that the donors were doing a favor to me or to the Gallery. After all, it is a spendid thing to be able to make a valuable gift to one's country, and to do it with discrimination and judgment.

It is the realization of this fact that has made the National Gallery what it is today. Congress has been generous in supplying funds for the operation of the Gallery, as it promised to do when the Gallery was established. But Congress has never been asked to buy a work of art for the National Gallery, nor has it been necessary to do so. The works of art in the Gallery have come from individuals and foundations; and these have included not only the Mellon, Kress, Widener, Dale, and Rosenwald Collections, but gifts from many individuals. Also it has been the Gallery's good fortune to have the interest and generosity of Mr. Mellon's son and daughter, Paul Mellon and the late Mrs. Ailsa Mellon Bruce. As can be seen in these pages, they have shown not only great generosity but imagination in realizing the Gallery's needs and in supplying funds for many activities and for works of art.

Fortunately there are many persons in this country who realize the importance of the art museum and also that it must grow in assets and services to the community in which it is located. If that growth is to be directed intelligently, the museum must be based on a definite philosophy and on a concrete, well-thought-out plan, adapted to the needs of the particular community but projected along lines that reach far into the future and are capable of being realized by degrees.

If we can make our art museums interesting and inviting places, where the public can enjoy the hours they spend there and become familiar with great works of art, or at least the best works of art procurable by the museum, then we have taken a long step forward in making the museum an essential part of modern life, as the university and the public library have long since become. As the museum becomes more and more necessary to an educated public, people generally will give it their support in order that they and their children may enjoy its benefits, along with those provided by other accepted institutions of learning.

It is only in the last hundred years that art museums in the United States have been in a position to render to the public services of the kind that I have described. Less than a hundred years ago American artists, such as Whistler, Sargent, and Mary Cassatt, felt obliged to go to France and England, Italy and Spain to study the great paintings which could be found there but not in their own country.

Today the National Gallery in Washington and many other American museums are in a position to do two things for which they were created; first to set up and maintain a standard of quality by collecting, preserving, and exhibiting to the best advantage the finest works of art obtainable in their chosen fields; and second, to make those works of art known and enjoyed by the people of this country and, indeed, by people everywhere to whom, in the larger sense, these and all works of art belong.

"Seeing," said Bernard Berenson, "is as much an acquired art as speaking, although no doubt easier to learn." Here the museum can be of help in leading one to an informed judgment, based on such facts and knowledge as are available through research and other means.

For most people the acquisition of such knowledge is largely a matter of self-education, once the discipline of school and university has been removed. And in education today the problem is the same as it has always been: to define the standards by which education is to be regulated. The museum is in a position to define, with some precision, the standard of excellence in art. To that extent it can provide a standard for education, at least in the field of the arts. And it also provides an opportunity for the average man and woman to learn something of the satisfying and enduring nature of cultural values, which neither time nor changing circumstances can take from them.

The museums and their related activities offer some of the few existing means to achieve that end. They can also help to give us "the privilege of an intelligent existence" by increasing our enjoyment and understanding of life. If they can succeed in doing that, they need no further justification for their existence or for the support, moral as well as financial, which they must have from the public whom they serve.

Index

Brearton, Joseph, 71
Brown, John Carter, 72, 172
Brown, John Nicholas, 160-161
Bruce, Ailsa Mellon (Mrs. David), 14, 35, 38, 57, 133, 135, 138, 144, 153, 173, 179
Bruce, David K. E., 14, 31, 42, 53, 56, 57, 58, 61, 69-70, 76, 98, 104, 127
Bruce, Mrs. Edward, 150
Burger, Warren E,. 76
Burke, William L. M., 160
Burroughs, Alan, 147
Buschbeck, Ernst, 86
Byrnes, James F., 76

C

Cahill, Holger, 137
Cairns, Huntington, 71, 105, 133, 142, 145-146, 159
Campbell, Ronald, 16
Carmichael, Leonard, 76
Carnegie-Mellon Institute, 147
Cassatt, Mary, 133
Chicago Art Institute, 110
Christensen, Erwin O., 137
Clark, Sir Kenneth (now Lord Clark of Saltwood), 144
Clark Collection (Corcoran Gallery of Art), 5
Clarke Collection (National Gallery of Art), 32, 48, 127
Commission of Fine Arts, 33, 150, 172
Concerts, National Gallery of Art, 151-152
Connally, John B., 76
Connally, Tom (Senator), 51
Cooke, Lester, 72
Coolidge, Calvin, 10, 13, 15
Corcoran, William Wilson, 5
Corcoran Gallery of Art, 5, 23, 173
Cott, Perry, 72
Credit-Anstalt Bank, Vienna, 16
Crittenden, Christopher, 138
Cromwell, William Nelson, Fund, 152
Crosby, Sumner McK., 159, 160
Cummings, Homer, 50
Curtis, Charles (Senator), 13-14

F

G

H

Knoedler, M., and Company, 9, 19, 22-23, 38
Knox, Philander C. (Senator), 10
Kress, Claude, 85
Kress, Rush H., 76, 78, 85 ff., 100, 168-169
Kress, Samuel H., 3, 37, 60, 62, 69, 76, 77 ff., 85, 103, 104, 168-169, 179
Kress, Samuel H., Collection, 4, 60, 61, 62, 63, 77 ff., 100, 103, 145, 168, 179
Kress, Samuel H., Foundation, 3, 77, 85, 89, 91, 146, 148, 168-169
Kress, Virginia (Mrs. Rush H.), 86

L

Laird, William S., 157
Laughlin, Irwin, 60-61, 64
Lee, Rensselaer W., 159-160
Lee, Ronald, 138
Leffingwell, Russell, 7
Legros' fountain, 64
Le Hand, Miss, 50
Lehman, Herbert H., 159
Leland, Waldo, 138
Lincoln, Abraham, 33
Lindsay, Sir Ronald, 31
Linnell, John, Collection, 119

M

McAdoo, William Gibbs, 7
McAneny, George, 138
McBride, Harry, 56, 70-71, 142, 155
McCray, Porter, 148
MacLeish, Archibald, 136, 159
Manet's *Old Musician*, 110
Maritain, Jacques, 144
Marriner, Theodore, 17
Marshall, George C., 76
Martin, Edward (Senator), 76
Medary, Milton B., 11
Mellon, André, 14
Mellon, Andrew W.
  personality of, 3-4, 8-9, 10
  Secretary of the Treasury, 3, 5, 7-8, 10
  gift of National Gallery building, 3, 6, 50

N

O

P

R

S

ABOUT THE AUTHOR. A native of York, South Carolina, David E. Finley is a graduate of the University of South Carolina, and received his law degree from George Washington University in 1913. He is the recipient of honorary doctorate degrees from both these institutions, and from Yale University (1946) and Georgetown University (1960).

Mr. Finley's long career in public service encompasses a variety of roles. After practicing law in Philadelphia, he served in the United States Army as a lieutenant during World War I. He was a member of the War Loan Staff of the United States Treasury Department from 1922, serving as Special Assistant to the Secretary of the Treasury, Andrew W. Mellon, from 1927 to 1932. In 1931 he married Margaret Morton Eustis. He held the position of honorary counselor at the American Embassy in London for one year during Mr. Mellon's Ambassadorship 1932-1933. From 1933-1937 Mr. Finley practiced law in Washington. In 1938 he was named first Director of the National Gallery of Art, a post he held until his retirement in 1956.

A member of the United States Commission of Fine Arts (1943–1950), Mr. Finley was Chairman from 1950–1963. Among many other membership positions, he has been Chairman, National Trust for Historic Preservation (1950–1962); and is presently Chairman, White House Historical Association; Trustee, Corcoran Gallery of Art; Member, National Portrait Gallery Commission and National Collection of Fine Arts Commission, Smithsonian Institution.

He is a recipient of the Theodore Roosevelt Distinguished Service Medal (1957), and the Henry Medal of the Smithsonian Institution (1964).